JOHN T. TRIGONIS

CROWD·FUNDING
for FILMMAKERS

THE WAY TO A SUCCESSFUL FILM CAMPAIGN

The World's Best-Selling Books for Independent Filmmakers

John has been a practitioner and teacher when it comes to crowdfunding. This book helps anyone learn from his experience. Readers will be empowered to turn their ideas into action and action into money and success.

— Slava Rubin, Founder & CEO, Indiegogo

Crowdfunding clearly isn't just about raising money. John thoroughly understands that it goes so much deeper than that, and with his practical, folksy wisdom, he explains everything you'd ever need to know about one of the most important things ever to hit the indie film world.

— Gregor Collins, Actor, Writer, Producer, *It's a Good Day to Die*

What do ancient Eastern philosophy and crowdfunding have in common? John knows and illustrates this connection wonderfully in *Crowdfunding for Filmmakers*, a very thorough look at not only crowdfunding, but social media, promotion, sales tactics, and so much more.

— Daniel Sisson, Daily Crowdsource

Chockfull of fantastic funding tips for your next movie by a filmmaker who has been through the process firsthand.

— Brian Meece, CEO of RocketHub

No one should begin a crowdfunding campaign without first reading John T. Trigonis' *Crowdfunding for Filmmakers*, which demystifies the crowdfunding process and ensures a successful campaign.

— Jayce Bartok, filmmaker, *The Cake Eaters* and blogger, *MovieMaker*; and Tiffany Bartok, filmmaker, *Tiny Dancer*

With wit and whimsy, John T. Trigonis successfully tackles the often intimidating subject of crowdfunding for filmmakers. Readers will appreciate the deft combination of thorough research, personal tribulations, and ancient Taoist wisdom that infuses the text. A must-read for any aspiring indie filmmaker looking to launch a crowdfunding campaign!

— Iri Greco, Co-Owner, BrakeThrough Media; V.P. Programs, New York Women in Film & Television

The world of crowdfunding can be confusing. After backing a friend's short film, I was daunted by where else to go. John was on hand to answer questions, offer advice, and guide me through the fun world of indie film. His guidance and crowdfunding philosophy proved invaluable. I have since backed nearly 200 successful projects, and I even co-ran my own campaign using the simple advice he had provided, which is now available in *Crowdfunding for Filmmakers* for everyone to read and follow.

— Gavin ap' Morrygan, Proud Producer, *The Saving, Cerise, Worst In Show, Crawl Bitch Crawl, Clowning Around*, and many others

Before learning about crowdfunding from John, I was an actor with a few unproduced screenplays. Now, I've got two features and two awards to my credit. In *Crowdfunding for Filmmakers*, John provides all the information he shared with me and more in a friendly, easy-to-read voice from one filmmaker to another.

> — Sam Platizky, Actor, Writer, and Producer, *Red Scare*, *Blaming George Romero*

As a full-time actor, sometimes DIY filmmaker, and president of the successful Golden Door International Film Festival of Jersey City, now in its third year, reading *Crowdfunding for Filmmakers* is like a breath of fresh air. John's depth of knowledge in the art of filmmaking (the Yin) is evident upon reading its first passage. What is so refreshing is his ability to leverage that knowledge and experience toward instructing us in dealing with the less desirable aspect of filmmaking — fundraising (the Yang). The points John makes about creating your crowdfunding campaign are so concise and easily applicable I feel juiced to start a campaign right away! *Crowdfunding for Filmmakers* is equal parts enjoyable, informative, and motivating.

> — Bill Sorvino, Actor, *A Place for Heroes*, *Pollination*

Whether you are a crowdfunding vet or considering your very first foray into this funding model, John T. Trigonis's *Crowdfunding for Filmmakers* should be among your resources for running a successful campaign.

> — Rick Vaicius, Founder and Executive Director, Flyway Film Festival

Everything we learned about #crowdfunding we learned from @Trigonis!

> — @IngeniousTheMovie, the indie film starring Jeremy Renner and Dallas Roberts

In a world where independent filmmaking is becoming more and more affordable, Trigonis gives you all the details on how to find and fund your latest project(s). The ins-and-outs and the ups-and-downs — they're all here.

> — Matthew Terry, Filmmaker, Screenwriter, and Teacher; Reviewer for *www.microfilmmaker.com*

Crowdfunding for Filmmakers is a timely book that is an easy and engaging read, giving a deep well of information for potential crowdfunders to tap into. The fact that it's written from a successful firsthand experience makes it all the better.

> — Erin Corrado, One Movie, Five Views

Trigonis leads the way to a painless and effective campaign. It's Zen and the Art of AUDIENCE Maintenance.

> — Kevin Sean Michaels, Director, Producer, *Ingrid Pitt: Beyond the Forest*

Crowdfunding for Filmmakers is worth the read. After all, your crowdfunding approach is what will make or break your film campaign.

> — Christopher Olenik, Founder and CEO, Agency | 2.0

CROWD FUNDING
FOR FILMMAKERS

THE WAY TO A SUCCESSFUL FILM CAMPAIGN

. . .

JOHN T. TRIGONIS

Published by Michael Wiese Productions
12400 Ventura Blvd. #1111
Studio City, CA 91604
tel. 818.379.8799
fax 818.986.3408
mw@mwp.com
www.mwp.com

Cover design: Johnny Ink www.johnnyink.com
Book interior design: Gina Mansfield Design
Editor: Gary Sunshine

Printed by McNaughton & Gunn, Inc., Saline, Michigan
Manufactured in the United States of America

Library of Congress Cataloging-in-Publication Data

Trigonis, John T.
 Crowdfunding for filmmakers : the way to a successful film campaign /
John T. Trigonis.
     p. cm.
 Includes bibliographical references and index.
 ISBN 978-1-61593-133-0
1. Motion pictures--Production and direction--United States. 2. Motion
picture industry--United States--Finance. 3. Investments--Technological
innovations--United States. I. Title.
 PN1995.9.P7T85 2013
 791.4302'33092--dc23
                                        2012027342

for Marinell

• • •

the meaning behind my every line

CONTENTS

ACKNOWLEDGMENTS

OVER THE YEARS I've met many talented filmmakers who not only make quality films and demonstrate an unbridled passion for the medium of the movies, but who have kept a keen eye on the future of filmmaking and film financing, and upon whose crowdfunding successes *Crowdfunding for Filmmakers* is based. To each of you — many of whom are mentioned numerous times throughout this book — I offer my deepest appreciation for your drive, innovation, and commitment to the art, craft, and business of making movies. Further thanks to Julie Keck and Jessica King, Gary King, Brendon Fogle, Jerry Cavallaro, Lucas McNelly, Andrew and Matt Rubin, and Joke and Biagio for being tremendously helpful in offering greater insight into each of their crowdfunding campaigns. I would also like to thank Slava Rubin and Danae Ringelmann of Indiegogo for their encouragement and unrivaled dedication to crowdfunding excellence.

An extra special thank you goes to my wonderful girlfriend, Marinell Montales, whose encouragement had originally pushed me to write the proposal for this book, which might have remained in my head indefinitely had it not been for her ardent belief in my words and that I am the right person to "write the book" on crowdfunding for filmmakers.

I would also like to thank my good friend, colleague, and mentor, Dr. James F. Broderick, for his sagely advice and helping me navigate the brave new world of publishing. To Alain Aguilar, Raul Garcia, Dani Shanberg, and Joe Whelski, best friends and partners in my diverse journey to create the next great work of imagination and wonder. And a special thanks to my family and especially the funders of my short film *Cerise*. Without their support, the mere thought of writing this book would never have crossed my mind.

Lastly, and with most gratitude, I would like to give a heartfelt thank you to Gary Sunshine for helping form a more complete harmony between my paragraphs and my ideas, and especially to Michael Wiese and Ken Lee at Michael Wiese Productions for making *Crowdfunding for Filmmakers* a reality.

PREFACE

WELCOME TO THE FUTURE OF FILM FUNDING

Crowdfunding for Filmmakers: The Way to a Successful Film Campaign is a book geared toward the everyday dreamer who has always wanted to pick up a camera and make a motion picture. It's for the Do-It-Yourselfer who's used to saving up $500 and gathering up a tribe of friends to shoot a YouTube video and who now wants to take video production to the next level. It's for the independent filmmaker who's made documentaries or narrative short and feature-length films through grants or investors and who now wants to stay on the cutting edge of not only filmmaking, but film financing as well. This book even goes far beyond the filmmaking front and can help visual artists, musicians, dancers, theater directors and playwrights, business startups, inventors, and many others raise the funds they need to bring their projects or products to the world.

But let's get back to filmmakers. Today, we don't have to be Hollywood studio executives to make films that look, sound, and feel like Hollywood blockbusters. The prime difference is money. The more we have, the more we can afford the talent and skills to make a masterpiece. Thankfully, the dawn of *crowdfunding* is upon us — reaching out to the crowd for the funds we need to make the movies we want to make and they want to watch. That said, this book caters to that community of indie filmmakers and moviegoers which seeks alternatives to the traditional, and crowdfunding has quickly become the preferred alternative to submitting scripts to studios, writing grant proposals, or finding investors who may only be concerned with a return on their investment. Crowdfunding levels the playing field between each of these extremes and allows the everyday Joe and Jane the opportunity to bring their creative projects to fruition.

And perhaps the best part is that you don't have to be a tech guru or marketing maven when it comes to crowdfunding. You don't have to have a degree in business, either, and you certainly won't get sued if you crowdfund (though you may want to check with your accountant when April rolls around so you can keep Uncle Sam at bay). What you do need is a deep-rooted passion for your film project and an uncompromising drive to move it from first page to scrolling credits. In terms of technology, all you really need is an email address, a Facebook profile, and a Twitter account, since these are the main methods by which you will obtain your funding — through rigorous online promotion. Other than that, all you need is a pinch of personalization and *Crowdfunding for Filmmakers* by your side, and you'll be on your way to cooking up a successful film campaign.

INTRODUCTION

THE *WHAT* OF CROWDFUNDING?

It's hard work making a movie. It's even harder securing the funds necessary to make one, especially at the independent level. Due to advancements in digital technology, just about anyone can afford a camera, be it a DSLR or a smart phone, and shoot a movie. Most Do-It-Yourself filmmakers learn their moviemaking skills through experience, wearing many different hats throughout the production process. The same goes for me. I've produced, written, directed, and edited eight of my own short films. Seven of those eight have been financed using my own money. No rich aunts, no lucky lottery numbers, just little amounts of money set aside here and there and lots of patience. But for one of my shorts, I decided to try something a little different, giving myself yet another title — *crowdfunder*.

Crowdfunding, one of the most popular alternatives to conventional methods of financing a film, is a form of online fundraising, in which a person sets up a project page, uploads a pitch video, offers some rewards, and reaches out directly to the audience through email and the social networks, as well as the more traditional modes of fundraising like word of mouth. In February of 2010, I launched a crowdfunding campaign for my short film *Cerise*. During the campaign, my team and I raised $6,300 in three months. That amount was $1,300 over our initial goal of $5,000, which we raised in two months by reaching out to the public through social networking via Facebook and Twitter, as well as by using the many tools afforded us by our crowdfunding platform of choice, Indiegogo.

A few months after my success crowdfunding *Cerise*, I wrote a trio of very popular blog posts under the umbrella of *The Tao of Crowdfunding*. My first post, "Three Ps for a Successful Film Campaign," received an inspiring write-up on *Indiewire.com*, which helped it garner 1,600 views in only one month. It's now up to over 3,200 views and counting. "A Practical Guide to Crowdfunder Etiquette," my second post, did equally well. But it was my third post, "Twitter Tips for Crowdfunders," featured on independent film producer and guru Ted Hope's blog Hope for Film, that made me realize that I've got the kind of practical knowledge of crowdfunding that can help point other filmmakers toward the kind of success I had with *Cerise*.

Why "the Tao" of crowdfunding? Taoism is an ancient Chinese philosophy developed by Lao Tzu. In his immortal work the *Tao Te Ching*, the "venerable master" expounds on the importance of always keeping the universe and oneself in proper balance, of going with the flow and not challenging it, and of embracing simplicity and gentleness above all else. In the *Tao Te Ching*, comprised of eighty-one short verses, Lao Tzu also reveals to his readers the main tenets of Taoism: *Tao* (the Way), *Te* (Integrity), *Pu* (the Uncarved Block), and the principle of *wu wei* (non-action).

So how does Taoism relate to crowdfunding? Through my firsthand experience as a crowdfunder, as well as a consultant and campaign analyst, I've found that when a campaigner remains true to the basic elements of fundraising — pitch, perks, and promotion — and enhances each of them with the fourth P — personalization — the chances of achieving over one's initial crowdfunding goal increase significantly. Therefore, *Crowdfunding for Filmmakers: The Way to a Successful Film Campaign* centers itself around the offering of practical information, tips, and tactics about how to launch and maintain a lucrative film campaign simply by going with the flow of traditional fundraising models and augmenting them with an added personal touch. The book examines various ways to meet and exceed one's crowdfunding goal through chapters that home in on team building, crowdfunder etiquette, and audience outreach, primarily through social media and other means of online promotion. You'll also find chapters containing case studies from successful and not-so-successful campaigns alike.

With lots of sound advice, solid examples, and the occasional tidbit of sagely insight from Taoist teacher Lao Tzu, *Crowdfunding for Filmmakers* will prove as enjoyable as it is informative and fully acclimate you to the brave new world of crowdfunding for independent film.

PART 1

FILM FINANCING
A BRIEF HISTORY

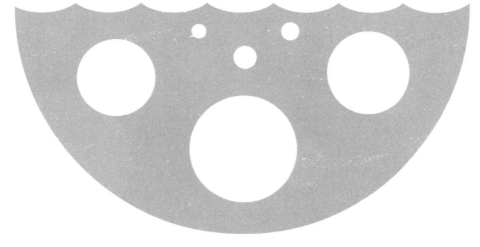

Chapter One

THE TRADITIONAL HOLLYWOOD MODEL OF FILM FINANCING

MAKING MOVIES IS SERIOUS BUSINESS.

The bulk of all that I know about Hollywood and how motion pictures are made comes from the silver screen. In classics like Billy Wilder's *Sunset Boulevard* and Nicholas Ray's *In a Lonely Place,* audiences are given a romanticized glimpse into the hustle-and-bustle, deadline-driven lifestyles of screenwriters. Preston Sturges' *Sullivan's Travels* takes the audience through an intense ride as a drama director who has struck a losing streak tries to regain his mojo and ultimately discovers an appreciation for comedy. And in *The Barefoot Contessa,* Humphrey Bogart and company take us on a tour of how directors, producers, and casting agents go about discovering new talent and casting movies.

What these classics don't show the general public is how these movies actually get made financially. That's the part that makes the movies such serious business. Blockbusters like *Prometheus* and *The Dark Knight Rises* aren't made with pocket change. It takes a lot of funds for Hollywood to put out the movies that it does. These movies are made by big studios like Paramount, MGM, and Warner Bros., using big money in the hopes of making that money back and earning a profit on this investment once the film is released theatrically to the public.

Today, the average movie can cost anywhere from $50 million to upward of $250 million. That's a far cry from back in the 1930s when a studio could produce a Hollywood picture for under $14 million. The 1939 classic *Gone with the Wind,* for instance, was made for between $3.9 and $4.25 million, according to Sheldon Hall and Stephen

Neale's book *Epics, Spectacles, and Blockbusters: A Hollywood History*. Cecil B. DeMille's classic *The Ten Commandments*, with its amazing special effects for the time, was made for $13.5 million, according to Tony Shaw's book *Hollywood's Cold War*.

Today, Hollywood produces motion-picture spectacles laden with computer generation and top billing, all at costs that tip over into the hundreds of millions. The first *Superman* film starring Christopher Reeve was made for around $55 million in 1978; twenty-eight years later *Superman Returns* was made for $209 million. At one time, costs were limited to lights, camera, film stock, the acquisition of rights if the film was an adaptation, and above-the-line expenses covering the director, writer, and actors. Studios still have to manage these costs nowadays, plus the costs of visual effects artists for films like *Pirates of the Caribbean*, which have budgets that can soar to near $300 million per picture. And these numbers just reflect the cost of production and do not include the costs of distribution, marketing, and promotion.

Again, making movies is serious business, and it's this kind of seriousness that has afforded the Hollywood studio system a powerful monopoly over not only the movie industry in the United States, but also the international entertainment industry. While I was at the Cannes Film Festival in 2011, I was stunned to see Johnny Depp's latest $250 million pirate escapade headlining alongside more artistic and less expensive films like *The Artist* ($12 million), which won the Academy Award for Best Picture that year, and *Midnight in Paris* ($17 million), a major contender for the same Oscar.

The independent film industry arose because of pioneers like Edward Burns, whose first film, *The Brothers McMullen*, cost an estimated $28,000 to shoot and launched an impressive and forward-thinking career for the New York native. But *The Brothers McMullen* was not the first independently produced film; arguably, *Star Wars* was produced in traditional indie fashion, meaning there was no studio backing for the film. This, of course, was before the term "independent" or "indie" went from simply meaning an alternative method of producing films to becoming its own film genre. After a slew of successful independently produced films had broken standard Hollywood tradition, studios like Sony, Fox, and NBCUniversal decided to subtly conquer this neutral territory by creating indie film companies like Sony Pictures Classics, Fox Searchlight, and Focus Features, respectively. After that, "independent" suddenly wasn't so indie anymore.

Thinking back to the days of *Sunset Boulevard* and *Sullivan's Travels*, it seems that if one wanted to be a screenwriter, a director, or even an actor, he or she would have to pick up and leave town for the neon lights of Los Angeles to nurture that dream into a reality. Flash forward to now, to a time when the all-powerful camera companies like Panasonic and Canon looked out and saw thousands of people all over the world who wanted to make movies, but because of Hollywood's iron grip on the entertainment industry, with all its beauties of fame and fortune, as well as its beasts of nepotism and cronyism, those dreamers didn't stand a chance at slipping a foot in the door. These camera companies ushered into the world the Dawn of the Digital Camera, and by doing so, gave rise to a new breed of truly independent filmmakers who all shouted in unison, "Let there be lights! Camera! Independence!"

•••

Chapter Two

THE DIY REVOLUTION

INDEPENDENCE, TOO, comes with its own set of costs. The fact is that not a lot of everyday Joes and Janes can wake up one morning and say "I want to make a film" and actually do it without having set aside a substantial amount of money for the endeavor. Ever since the independent movement emerged from the trenches of World War II, ordinary people have been able to buy inexpensive portable cameras, shoot footage, and splice it together into a film. But even the people whom filmmakers tend to immortalize as the founding fathers of indie film — namely Dennis Hopper (*Easy Rider*), Francis Ford Coppola (*Apocalypse Now*) and George Lucas (*THX 1138* and, of course, *Star Wars*) — already had established names in the industry. But what about all the nameless filmmakers out there, the ones who have no connections, no desire to leave their lives behind for the star-paved promenade of Hollywood Boulevard? How do these filmmakers grab hold of a chance at possibly being the next Stanley Kubrick or Edward Burns?

The term "independent" has gone through a metamorphosis and no longer means independent. It's natural, after all; a stock boy doesn't continue stocking shelves after he's been promoted to general manager. Even the prestigious Sundance Film Festival, which once upon a time served as a haven for indie filmmakers, has itself become a celebrity stalking ground, attracting studio films and those made by well-known indie personalities, as well as films from that neighborhood dreamer who shot his or her first movie on a smart phone and ponied up the $60 submission fee.

Now, this new incarnation of indie filmmakers, once only dreamers, has been granted the tools necessary to make their own films with newfound ease. Filmmakers like my best friend, Alain Aguilar, who dared to dream of one day making motion pictures. He didn't have to dream very long. The year he decided to pursue filmmaking was the same year Canon unveiled its XL-1 Mini-DV camcorder. Alain saved up the $2,500 needed to buy the camera to make his first film, *Cog*. We shot the film, edited it, added music, and eventually got it screened at NewFilmmakers NY.

But having a consumer-grade digital camera doesn't turn someone into an indie filmmaker overnight, especially if one's film costs nothing to produce. How can anyone make a film with no money? Easy: make it with friends, something that just about every beginning filmmaker does. No one was paid on the set of *Cog*, either in front of the camera or behind it. I not only wrote the film, but I also starred as the main character. The location was Alain's workplace on the weekend; the food was leftovers in the fridge that his coworkers hadn't eaten; Alain edited the film using Adobe Premiere, which his company owned; and the music was public domain — if Beethoven's Ninth Symphony was good enough for Kubrick, it'd be good enough for us. This was not independent filmmaking in any way. Yes, we were just as independent from the Hollywood studio system and their $100 million budgets as Edward Burns and Kevin Smith were, but without even the slightest amount of money to qualify as "independent," we couldn't really classify ourselves as indie filmmakers. A typical independent film budget runs around $500,000 to $1 million. Most filmmakers like Alain and myself don't have access to that kind of cash to invest in a motion picture. Filmmakers like us do it run-and-gun, guerilla-style, or what has become more commonly referred to as Do-It-Yourself (DIY).

DIY filmmakers have an advantage today that they didn't have back in the late 1990s or early 2000s. A camera is the most essential piece of equipment one needs to make a film, and today filmmakers can acquire most topnotch cameras at very reasonable costs. The XL-1 was the height of 3CCD technology when Alain and I used it to film

Cog. When I shot my short film *Perfekt* in 2005, we used Panasonic's HVX200, which was one of the first prosumer grade high-definition cameras on the market and was revered because of its ability to save files directly onto Panasonic's patented P2 cards instead of mini-DV tapes. Now, aside from Red and 3D camera technology, many films are shot using Digital SLRs like the Canon 7D, available for a mere $1,500, its younger brother the T3i, a steal at slightly under $1,000, and the 5D Mark III for around $3,000.

If an aspiring filmmaker really can't afford those amounts, he or she can always shoot a decent short film or feature-length movie using an iPhone or other mobile device that captures HD images, and from there, it can easily be edited on iMovie for upload or export. In this sense, the DIY filmmaker has true independence. But good content — be it DIY, independent, or Hollywood — usually costs something to make, and that dollar amount doesn't stop at the price of a camera upgrade from a Droid to a Sony EX-3. For larger films, you'll need a larger crew since there are limitations to working with friends, especially if they are working for free pulling cables because they don't know much about how films are put together.

The need for money to make films doesn't stop at production funds. Later you may need editing or After Effects work done on your film that you yourself can't do. Or perhaps some CGI will need to be incorporated. Perhaps the audio will need some adjustments. Sure, you can learn all of this yourself and implement these changes, but let's be honest — nothing spells "amateur" like seeing your name under almost every credit from "Writer/Director" to "Gaffer" and "Music by." Do-It-Yourself doesn't really mean that you literally do everything yourself; on the contrary, you do it yourself because you want to be the person with control over what the finished film will be, which means you're the person who casts, hires crew, and performs all the other producer tasks that will make your film a success or a forgotten dream.

That said, even the DIY filmmaker can't avoid having to find the funds necessary to make his or her film the best it can be. You can do what I've done for seven of my eight short films and wait a year or so working a day job and setting aside some of your savings for your $2,000 or $100,000 motion picture to happen. You can write up a few grant proposals and mail them off, then sit and wait for the boards and committees to decide whether to pay up or pass on your film idea. You can even try and find private-sector investors and hope they'll provide some substantial amounts, which you will more than likely need to pay back.

Or you can play it smart, be ahead of the times, and raise the funds you need for your film while at the same time build an audience for and awareness of your finished product. This way, you not only get funding for your film project, but you also have an audience that wants to see your film once it's finished because they helped pay for it.

Filmmaking, meet crowdfunding.

Chapter Three

• • •

CROWDFUNDING AND FILMMAKING: YIN MEETS ITS YANG

FILMMAKING HAS BEEN CAUGHT in a state of flux over the last ten years. The dawn of the digital camera has spawned a new breed of truly independent, DIY filmmaker rooted in the ideals of guerilla filmmaking. The advent of HD and 3D technology has given rise to a "Do It Yourself Revolution," granting these innovative moviemakers the same image quality and versatility that Hollywood's Stevens Spielberg and Soderbergh achieve in their big-budget blockbusters. So it's only natural to think that if these filmmakers were granted even the smallest fraction of a studio-sized budget, they might be able to create quality indie films at Hollywood caliber, but not at Hollywood costs.

Enter crowdfunding, a phenomenon that's been around since the 1990s, which serves as an alternative method of raising capital for creative projects. The concept is fairly simple: by launching a campaign on one of the crowdfunding platforms like Indiegogo, Kickstarter, and the more than 400 others sprawled throughout the Internet, filmmakers can now go directly to the crowd for the money they need to make their films, and with a few clicks of a mouse, anyone can contribute money to those film projects with ease.

Crowdfunding is modeled after the "rewards system." Campaigns will include a pitch video, which usually informs the crowd about the filmmaker and the nature of his or her particular project, and provides a list of perks extended to potential contributors in exchange for giving money. The crowdfunding platforms serve as intermediaries that help out with this kind of online fundraising by offering important features like easy payment options through PayPal or Amazon and the integration of social networking, making it easy for filmmakers and their supporters to promote their film projects to their friends and other prospective contributors.

Despite reaching a critical mass of sorts in the late 2000s, the concept of crowdfunding can be traced back as far as the 1700s, its origins rooted in the earliest forms of microfinancing. The first time I ever heard about crowdfunding was when documentary filmmaker Gregory Bayne crowdfunded the money he needed to finish his feature-length documentary *Jens Pulver: Driven*. With a lot of hard work and constant social networking, he raised $27,210 on Kickstarter. This impressive victory made waves in the indie film community because Gregory was also able to generate such a staggering amount of funding in less than one month from 410 backers — mostly fellow filmmakers and everyday people who had an interest in movies and mixed martial arts, the target audience for the film.

Since Gregory's triumph with *Jens Pulver: Driven*, many other DIY filmmakers have followed in his footsteps. Some successfully crowd-funded projects include:

- Phil Holbrook's feature-length thriller *Tilt* ($15,606 of $15,000 on Kickstarter)

- Brendon Fogle's short film *Sync* ($3,405 of $3,000 on Indiegogo)

- John Paul Rice's social issue feature *Mother's Red Dress* ($20,678 of $20,000 on Kickstarter)

- Sam Platizky's zombie comedy *Red Scare* ($7,645 of $7,500 on Indiegogo)

- Tim Attewell's sci-fi short *Gateway* ($5,907 of $5,000 on Kickstarter)

- Damien Cullen's short comedy *Clowning Around* ($8,900 of $7,500 on Indiegogo)

- Joke and Biagio's feature-length documentary *Dying to Do Letterman* ($55,140 of $37,000 on Kickstarter)

- Charles Simon's web series *Duhmfownd* ($1,600 of $1,300 on Indiegogo)

- Jocelyn Towne's feature-length film *I Am I* ($111,965 of $100,000 on Kickstarter)

There is also up-and-coming auteur Gary King's movie musical *How Do You Write a Joe Schermann Song*, which initially raised $31,101, then raised an additional $18,031 in a second campaign for finishing funds via Kickstarter. Then there's the come-from-behind win of Lucas McNelly's *A Year Without Rent*, in which 75% of its $12,178 total was raised in the final days and hours of his Kickstarter campaign — a true testament to the power of the crowd as a serious alternative to traditional film financing.

Since all of these campaigns raised over their initial fundraising goals, it's easy to see that crowdfunding is not a passing fad, but a burgeoning revolution. In simpler, more Eastern terms, the yin of DIY filmmaking seems to have found its yang in crowdfunding. The yin yang, or *Taijitu*, is the primary symbol of the ancient Chinese philosophy of Taoism and represents the balance between opposing forces. In this case, those opposing forces are filmmaking and film funding. Neither of them can exist without each other. You can't make a top-quality film with-

out some funding; by the same token, you can have all the money in the world, but if you lack the skills necessary to actually make a film, that money will be sadly misspent.

By carefully examining various campaigns over the years, as well as revisiting my own experiences crowdfunding my short film *Cerise*, I've found that some people do it right, and others do not. Rather, they work harder, not smarter. I

The Taijitu *is the Chinese symbol representing the concept of yin and yang, the balance and harmony in the universe.*

realized that most filmmakers don't consider themselves crowd-funders, never mind entrepreneurs, and therefore don't take time beforehand to research other campaign strategies like I had done and instead navigate this new landscape with a blindfold and a prayer. But this particular dream, in order to be realized, must always be seen with clarity throughout the duration of the journey we're about to begin.

· PART ONE ·
SUMMARY POINTS

- During the Golden Age of Studio Films, Hollywood made big-budget films using its own in-house funds, shooting on the lot while hoping to clean up at the box office and recoup its initial investment, plus plenty of profit.

- In the Silver Age of Indie Film Financing, low-budget indie movies were financed using money from grants, private sector investors, the oftentimes difficult-to-secure distribution deal, and the film-makers' own savings.

- The Crowdfunding Age of Do-It-Yourself Filmmaking is upon us, which makes it easier for everyday filmmakers to go to the crowd and seek the funding they need to make their truly independent films a reality.

· PART ONE ·
EXERCISES

1. Think about some Hollywood blockbusters you've seen recently. Pick three of your favorites and research how much each one cost to produce. Then, do the same for three independent films of your choice. Compare the quality, the content, and the cost of each.

2. Take a look at a few movies or web series on YouTube or Vimeo. How do they stack up in terms of quality, content, and especially cost, to the three indie films you chose in exercise one? How about your three Hollywood blockbusters?

3. Based on the above comparisons, start thinking about your own short or feature-length film. What kind of content do you want to put out into the world? What's the quality you want to achieve? How much might it cost you to achieve it?

PART 2 CROWD FUNDING BASICS

Chapter Four

• • •

TAO: BEGIN WITH THE BASICS OF FUNDRAISING

ACCORDING TO THE *Tao Te Ching*, the word Tao (pronounced as Dao) means "the Way," and that way usually means going with the natural flow of the universe. So why might anyone want to deviate from that ideology in any other aspect of life, especially where raising money is concerned? The fact is that many of us choose "the road less taken" to get to where we want to be in life, and that's fine, but only after you've taken care of the basics, which oftentimes do not change.

Certain elements of traditional fundraising should be implemented into one's crowdfunding campaign before getting into all the innovation and trial and error of this very contemporary technique. These aspects have been in place since the dawn of fundraising, and like nature, they are pretty much constant. They include essentials like building a solid team, deciding how much funding you need for your project, gearing your campaign toward a target audience, and forming and maintaining a campaign strategy. Without any of these elements fixed in place and clearly identified, you risk going against the natural ways of raising money and will no doubt find yourself working harder, not smarter.

Perhaps the only aspect that is new to the established model of fundraising is the idea of a crowdfunding intermediary through which a person runs his or her campaign. Fundraising has been around long before the age of the Internet, and so has crowdfunding. One of the very first crowdfunded projects was the Statue of Liberty back in 1882, when Joseph Pulitzer turned to the American people to help raise the additional $150,000 to finish construction of the pedestal on which it would stand. So although the Internet was not part of the natural flow of fundraising back then, it has quickly become a vital part of crowdfunding.

These next few chapters are all about going with the current that's been flowing strongly for hundreds of years so you can carefully plot out your film campaign and come out of it with few, if any, battle scars. But, as the very first line of the *Tao Tê Ching* boldly states, "The Tao that can be told is not the eternal Tao," keep in mind that this is by far not the only way to run a successful crowdfunding campaign, nor can anyone truly say any way is the right way. It is simply the way that many successful film campaigns go about the process, the same way I went about it when I crowdfunded *Cerise*, and the same way you should undertake crowdfunding for your film project.

Chapter Five

• • •

DECIDE IF CROWDFUNDING IS RIGHT FOR YOUR FILM PROJECT

THE FIRST AND MOST IMPORTANT THING you must decide as a filmmaker is whether crowdfunding is right for your particular film project. Other questions that will more than likely follow will be whether you have enough time to properly launch and effectively run a campaign for two or three months and if you have enough initial support for such an endeavor. We'll revisit those last two questions later. For now, let's focus on one key aspect that most filmmakers don't realize is a pivotal starting point for making the decision to crowdfund a film project.

In order to launch a successful crowdfunding campaign, it helps to accept the fact that during the one to three months or more of online fundraising for your film project, you are no longer a filmmaker, but a crowdfunder. A crowdfunder, by definition, is someone fully focused on raising money from the crowd for a project he or she will ultimately share with that crowd. In other words, if your script isn't finished, or if you're in the middle of preproduction, or if you're still coming up with a great idea to shoot, crowdfunding is probably not in your best interest at the moment.

The phrase that follows will be repeated many times throughout this book, and with good cause — it is an absolute, unwavering truth: *Crowdfunding is a full-time job.* Anyone who claims otherwise probably doesn't have a successful campaign under his or her belt. Therefore, whether crowdfunding is right for your film project is partly dependent on your ability to temporarily minimize the Final Draft window on your screenplay, bookmark your *Cinematographer's Handbook*, and focus your full attention on fundraising. If you can do this, then we can take a deeper look at the question of whether your specific film or video project should be crowdfunded, and that answer rests primarily with how much money you actually need to make your film.

As of this writing, no crowdfunded film or video project has raised over $1 million, but there are plenty of film projects that have raised amounts in the hundreds of thousands of dollars, which is a very impressive feat. But Hollywood films cannot be made on a shoestring budget; if your project calls for plenty of expensive computer graphics to tell its story, or requires locations that are difficult to secure, then crowdfunding may not be the best option for you.

Another reason most people may not opt for crowdfunding and instead start saving their own money or pursue more traditional approaches like submitting scripts to independent studios, writing grant proposals, and seeking the aid of private sector investors, is that they don't believe they have the support system to make a crowdfunding campaign successful. This, however, is a bit of resistance working its way into the mind. In truth, not many DIY filmmakers have the support of hundreds or thousands of people who might each contribute a dollar to your campaign, but that's where the idea of crowdfunding being a full-time job comes into play. You'll have to work hard to increase your initial support system. Its foundation will most likely be comprised of family and friends, which is normal because if they won't back you on your project, who else will? Then, once you start promoting on the Internet, specifically through social networking sites, you'll slowly but surely begin building a larger following and stronger fan base for your film.

It also helps to know that there are certain types of films that fare better in the crowdfunding circuit than others. Most documentaries, for instance, do extremely well, not only because they deal with real stories of real people, but also because many times documentarians can reach out to particular groups, organizations, and institutions for further support and contributions. Campaigns for narrative films may require more innovative and creative tactics to appeal to random people and make them contribute. This is where a compelling pitch and unique perks come into play.

Genre, too, can play a significant role in your crowdfunding efforts. By genre, I don't necessarily mean attaching the term "independent" to your campaign — the fact that you're crowdfunding is statement enough for its independence. Rather, is your film a horror film? Action/adventure? Romantic comedy? Some genres do better than others, but more important than genre is your niche audience — that very specific audience you're going to home in on most. Hollywood makes romantic comedies and sci-fi films (genres), but indie filmmakers make stoner comedies and social issue films (niches), which cater to very particular groups of people.

But before this, you will want to make certain there is an audience for your film, and the good news is that in today's world, there's an audience for every film. You simply have to tap into your niche and genre and focus your pitch, perks, and promotion heavily on them. Oftentimes, that also means targeting a specific demographic. For instance, if you narrow down your audience from horror movie fans, which may be a bit too vague, to Asian-American (demographic) hardcore (niche) horror (genre), you may be more likely to build a massive awareness of your film within the population most likely to buy into your film.

Another question to ask yourself is whether you can make your crowdfunding campaign relevant to your film's content. This is a question overlooked by many crowdfunders, but I find it's extremely important. People like details, and it's human nature for us to look for patterns and connections in everything we see and experience. You should be able to tie your crowdfunding tactics directly or indirectly into your campaign. My short film *Cerise* is about a former spelling bee champion who's haunted by the word that took him down. The movie deals with words, so whenever possible, my campaign was centered around words, whether in the form of poetry-infused perks or spelling bees on Twitter. The more you can connect your project to your campaign, the more your contributors will keep your project in their minds, from its crowdfunding campaign to its film festival premiere.

Is there any truth to the statement that crowdfunding is right for certain projects but not for others? Yes and no. It all depends on your answers to the above questions, as well as whether you'll be able to nurture and sustain a desire in the audience to see your film once it's finished. This is very similar to marketing a finished film using a trailer. Once you watch the trailer for a movie like *The Dark Knight Rises*, the video has gone viral on YouTube by the next second, has been plastered all over Facebook and Twitter by your friends and followers within an hour, and by the end of the day, it's been reviewed by comic book and movie blogs across six continents. And why? Well, it's Batman, of course! But aside from that, a desire was created in people to want to see this film. With crowdfunding, your aim is to evoke a similar response in your contributors, but instead of a trailer, you have a pitch. Instead of the finished film, you have a film that needs to be made, along with the passion and drive to make it. It's a challenge, but the tougher the challenge, the greater the reward.

Crowdfunding comes with its own set of challenges, which is why it helps to not look at it entirely through the eyes of a filmmaker, as it's far too easy to slip into the old-fashioned "starving artist" sentiment or declare that crowdfunding is not for you because you might be too proud or timid to ask others for money. On the other hand, you shouldn't approach crowdfunding 100% like an entrepreneur either, as it's equally easy to fall into the chasm of the egocentric businessperson. The *Tao* of crowdfunding is about balance and harmony between these two seemingly opposing forces, making the process not about you, but about your contributors and, most importantly, your film.

Chapter Six

• • •

BUILD YOUR TEAM

HOW IMPORTANT IS HAVING A TEAM of like-minded people when you begin your crowdfunding campaign? A better question might be this: Can you make a film all by yourself? Sure you can; with a mobile phone or DSLR, you can make a perfectly fine short film that could be the next smash hit on YouTube, but no one will give you $10,000 to make it. Quality DIY filmmaking is a team effort. The only difference between DIY and Hollywood is money and manpower. When a blockbuster like Ridley Scott's *Prometheus* ends, the credits go on seemingly forever, and we as audience members see how many people it actually takes to put together a 124-minute-long movie for our enjoyment. By contrast, when we see a film and every third credit names the same person, we know that it was made on the cheap, which often translates to the film being of mediocre-to-poor quality.

To be taken more seriously as a filmmaker, eventually we learn that we have to start bringing people on board our projects who know how to handle all the aspects of filmmaking that may not be our strongest suit. The same applies to crowdfunding. It's a full-time job to get from $0 to $10,000, and though you could do it alone, why would you? You'll be doing more work than you need to, which means you'll be going against the natural way of things and breaking a major tenet of Taoism, which we'll discuss in Chapter Twenty-Six. Plus, part of your crowd will be composed of your own teammates, who will take on certain responsibilities while you focus on others. And according to data available through Indiegogo, if you have four or more members on your team, you'll raise 70% more money than if it were only you running your campaign.

When I started my campaigning for *Cerise*, there were only two members of my team: my girlfriend, Marinell, and myself. Ultimately, we brought in Alain, the film's cinematographer, and Nino Rajacic, the musician who scored the film. How many members of this team did the bulk of the work? Two. Alain sent out a few Tweets and status updates here and there, as did Nino, which opened up to us a slightly wider reach, but it was Marinell and myself who tackled the majority of the promotion, and that was fine, because every little bit adds to the crowdfunding effort.

The fact is that by showing there is more than just one member of your team, you build more credibility in the minds of potential contributors, making them think that this particular project may be more serious than another film campaign being run by a pair of high school kids. Crowdfunding is about community, and community starts with you and those closest to you. However modest it may be at first, there should be a team firmly in place so that others will take initiative and join your growing community.

Having a team is important, and in hindsight, I would've benefited greatly by having a somewhat larger team than my Fab Foursome for *Cerise*, and some who were more adept with things like social media. Marinell was the only one except myself who helped keep the campaign active on Facebook and Twitter. But Marinell has a Bachelor of Science degree in marketing and a passion for film, so she was able to handle most of the creative marketing and promotional planning for the campaign, which was one less thing I had to think about. I just had to help carry out those plans. It's not important to simply have a team of people listed on your film campaign's homepage; when possible, they should be the right people, those who have specific skills and who will prove an asset all along your campaign trail and help maximize its potential for success.

BRING YOUR ACTORS AND CREW ABOARD

Crowdfunding is not only about raising money and awareness. It's also about showing support, and you will look well supported if you bring your actors and crew into your campaign. This can also include the various producers who will no doubt want to have their names listed not only in the credits of the film but also on your campaign's homepage for all the world to see. Take a look at this Indiegogo campaign for *We Are the Hartmans*, a feature-length film about a rock music nightclub that's about to be sold by its owners until they are greeted by a full-scale rebellion by the local rock bands that have played the venue. There are fourteen teammates in total, mostly actors in the film, co-producers, and the film's director.

The whole Hartmans *team pitches in to make the campaign a success.*

Something else you may notice is that Team Hartman and Cielito Pascual are not only co-producers and handling the marketing for the campaign and the film, but they are also responsible for

"FUNdraising." This is a very simple tactic, but it shows potential contributors that the filmmakers behind *We Are the Hartmans* are not only all about raising money to finish the film, but they are also determined to have a good time doing it and share that good time with their funders.

BRING ON YOUR OTHER SUPPORTERS

Another effort that focused some attention on bringing on additional team members is the Indiegogo campaign for Charles Simons' web series *Deader Days*, a zombie comedy about a zombie named Daryl who's trying to fit in with the living. The campaign features actors' names along with a brief description of the characters they play (e.g., Jayce Basques, who plays Daryl, "your friendly neighborhood Zombie"), as well as crewmembers from writer/director down to the gaffer. But Charles, the executive producer, also got more creative and downright playful with the titles of those team members who aren't necessarily a direct part of the production, but who are no doubt a supportive force for *Deader Days*.

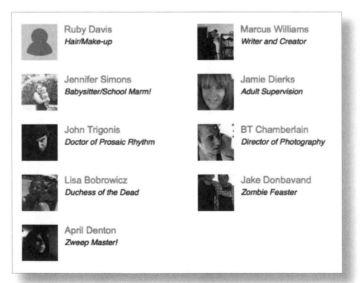

Creative titles like "Zweep Master" make campaigning for Deader Days *even more playful.*

Titles like "Duchess of the Dead" and "Zweep Master" add a sense of silliness to this darkly comedic series. Charles even gave me a title since I helped him promote his prior Indiegogo success story — another web series called *Duhmfownd* — as well as on *Deader Days*. I was branded "Doctor of Prosaic Rhythm" due to my tendency to Tweet very original messages about the project and because of my job as a professor.

Whether your team is comprised of actors and crew, friends and family, or just everyday people who are being recognized for their support, the more assistance you have, the more authenticity you gain as a serious filmmaker and force to be reckoned with, as well as someone worth giving money to.

SKILLS. SKILLS. SKILLS.

Sometimes the greatest actor can make a mediocre director, and not many writers can apply their storytelling finesse with words to the cuts and dissolves a good editor makes use of to tell a more visual story. The same holds true with regard to crowdfunding. When giving members of your team tasks to handle during your campaigning efforts, it's helpful to make sure that those jobs correspond with the skill set they already have. If a person doesn't have a Facebook account by the time your campaign starts, you shouldn't realistically expect him or her to promote the campaign in that way because it's foreign and therefore will take some time to get the swing of it and build a network.

If a person has a good eye for graphics and design, on the other hand, let him or her handle all of the designing for the campaign, such as Facebook profile pictures and cover photos, newsletter designs, and poster art. If another person has a large filmmaker network on Twitter, it's a safe bet that he or she should be able to get word out about your film project and garner contributions much more effectively than someone who's only a "Social Tweeter" according to their low Klout Score. Always fit the appropriate responsibility to the most skilled person for the job, and you won't go wrong when choosing the right team because you'll simply be going with its own flow.

Chapter Seven

• • •

DECIDE HOW MUCH FUNDING YOU NEED

KEEPING WITH THE NATURAL FLOW of the *Tao* of fundraising, after you've pieced together your initial team to help drive traffic to your film's campaign homepage, you should figure out exactly how much funding you'll need to bring your film from script to screen. This means doing some legwork and figuring out specifically what your film needs money for. The more accurate you can be, the better. Rough guestimates probably won't be enough; remember, you're asking random people for money to help you with your project, and people seldom part with their money without knowing the details.

Most people want to know exactly where their hard-earned money will go or what it will be used for. That's an everyday life thing, and crowdfunding is no exception, especially since there are more ordinary people out there contributing to indie film projects than there are Jerry Bruckheimers. You'll have to let your potential contributors know what their money will be spent on, which means you need to know that information first.

BE UPFRONT WITH POTENTIAL CONTRIBUTORS

A general statement about what the funds you're raising will be used for should suffice for most people, so you don't have to get as detailed as a full-fledged budget breakdown, since most regular Joes and Janes won't read it. If you're raising money for the production, it may not be the best thing to state that "the money will go to all aspects of the production." That's too vague, and someone who may not know a thing about the filmmaking process could get deterred from contributing because you haven't offered any tangible information. If you state that the funds will go to pay the actors and crew and feed them, you'll be more likely to attract a contribution from a random person. If you're raising money for postproduction expenses like ADR or editing, mention that as well, because it's much more understandable to the average person than the word "postproduction."

When I was crowdfunding for *Cerise*, Indiegogo actually had a section called "How These Funds Will Be Used," which had to be filled out by all campaigners. I thought this was a very helpful feature for both crowdfunders and contributors. Had it not been there, I may have erroneously thought that crowdfunders didn't necessarily have to tell people exactly what the money would be used for, or that I didn't need to mention it in detail because everyone probably knows how films are made. Both of these assumptions are simply not valid. Indiegogo has since removed this feature and now leaves it up to the individual crowdfunders to include that information somewhere on their campaign pages. I look at plenty of crowdfunding campaigns, and I see a lot of nebulous descriptions like this one for Sean King's Indiegogo campaign for his web series *The Gumshoe*: "$9,000 is need [sic] to produce the pilot, which includes four days of filming in Los Angeles, post-production and marketing." Words like "postproduction" and "marketing" are way too imprecise for those of us who know little to nothing about either of them.

Here are a few examples of campaigns that have explained what contributions to their film projects will be going toward. First, producer John Paul Rice keeps visitors to his Kickstarter page for his social-issue feature *Mother's Red Dress* from seeing red by bullet-pointing his funding needs. He starts out with a general note that "the funds raised will be used to complete the film now in post-production," but then delves into specifics, from hiring a sound mixer "who can deliver the quality of sound you hear when seeing a movie in theaters" to a visual effects artist who will "create all those incredible images seen in movies." He also includes examples and a link to a color correction demo on Vimeo so that people understand how important their contributions are.

Next, Finnish filmmaker Jukka Vidgren goes one step further and puts some pretty exact estimates on his Indiegogo campaign for his short motion novel *Dr. Professor's Thesis of Evil*. For some people, it helps to see the numbers and know that renting a sound studio costs $2,600 and actor and travel fees would run up a serious $4,600, since Jukka has to hire English-speaking actors, which means looking to England and the U.S. for talent and flying them to Finland to record the voiceovers of this short cinematic work.

This information should be kept all together and in one place on your film campaign's homepage so it's easier for potential contributors to locate, especially if you include a heading to help catch their attention, such as "What We Need and What You Get." The goal is to make your campaign information easily accessible so people will reach into their hearts and wallets more quickly, helping you and your film to the finish line.

WHAT IF I RAISE MORE MONEY THAN I ASKED FOR?

It happens. Let's say you're crowdfunding for $30,000 to bring to life your ninety-page script and you end up raising $35,000. Do you keep it? Of course you do! Most likely, you're raising the minimum amount of money you'll need to make the film you want to make, so if you get a little or a lot extra, you can do that much more with it for your film. I do suggest letting your contributors know what exactly you'll be doing with the additional funding, of course, since it is other people's money you're making your movie with, and they deserve to know what it's going to be spent on.

With *Cerise*, the target goal was set at $5,000, and I ended up making it in only two months. My team and I had an extra month to raise more money, but I decided not to actively raise it because I had also saved $10,000 of my own for *Cerise*. "If more money comes in, then let it," I told my teammates. It certainly did come in — an additional $1,300 without my sending out a single Tweet, status update, or email blast. As a result, I ended up coming in below budget and used that money saved to pay our production assistants a small stipend since they were all working for experience.

In DIY filmmaking, there's no such thing as too much money, and there will always be something worthwhile to spend that additional money on.

Chapter Eight

• • •

CHOOSE YOUR PLATFORM

YOUR CROWDFUNDING PLATFORM is your campaign's starting point, much like the platform you stand on while waiting to catch a subway or train. It's your hub, your Grand Central Station, and every train you send out along the rails of the Internet — the Twitter Express, the Facebook Local — will ultimately direct your potential contributors back to that starting point. A crowdfunding platform is a website that aids in the fundraising process by offering crowdfunders a space to host their campaign and supplying them with the tools necessary to promote on the Internet. Although there are over 400 such intermediaries like RocketHub, Ulule, and Crowdfunder, this book will focus its attention on Indiegogo and Kickstarter, the two powerhouses that have become synonymous with crowdfunding and are used by more filmmakers than any other platform.

A quick glimpse at Indiegogo and Kickstarter, as well as any other crowdfunding platform, will reveal certain similarities. At the top of a campaign's homepage, you'll find the project title and a logline or other brief description of the project. Below is the pitch video, through which you, the crowdfunder, will pitch your film project to the crowd. To the right of the pitch video is where you'll find the perks, what your contributors get in exchange for their monetary support of your project. These three elements make up the basics of crowdfunding, but aside from these constants, there are also important differences that you as a crowdfunder need to think about before choosing which platform is right for you and your film project.

ALL OR NOTHING VS. ALL OR MORE

It is essential to keep a positive outlook and believe without a doubt that you will reach your crowdfunding goal. But even the firmest belief casts a subtle shadow: *What if I don't make it?* One of the most important things to consider when choosing a platform is whether by the end of it you want to walk away with some or no money in the event of an unsuccessful campaign, or what's known in the crowdfunding community as "All or Nothing" or "All or More" deadlines. In the "All or Nothing" model, primarily used by Kickstarter, if you don't reach your goal by your set deadline, you don't get to keep any of the funds you spent all those months raising; so if your target is set at $15,000 for your feature-length comedy and you only raise $14,500, you get nothing for your efforts.

In the "All or More" model, popularized by Indiegogo, if you don't raise the entire $15,000 for your film and instead only raise $5,000 by your deadline, you get to keep the $5,000 you did earn. But if you do reach your $15,000 goal, you get rewarded. Since crowdfunding platforms have to make money to keep offering their services, they charge their users a percentage on the money that's earned. Kickstarter takes a fixed fee of 5% only when you reach your goal. With Indiegogo, however, if you don't reach your goal, you pay 9% of the total funds you earned, but if you do reach or exceed your goal, Indiegogo only takes 4%, so it's in your best interest to reach your goal.

There are pros and cons to each of these models. The "All or Nothing" variety may seem like too much of a risk, and many filmmakers, particularly those who may not have a strong enough fan base to guarantee a successful campaign, might shy away from this. Others view it in a very positive way, as it adds a certain sense of immediacy to a campaign, which makes people more inclined to contribute right away instead of waiting and perhaps hoping the crowdfunder makes his or her goal before they get the chance to type in their credit card numbers.

Something else to consider when choosing a platform is when the money is taken from the contributor and disbursed to the crowd-funder. When a funder clicks the "Contribute Now" button on Indiegogo, for instance, that $25 he or she gives to a film project is taken out of their account or credit card immediately, whereas with Kickstarter, the backer's information is taken and held until there's a green banner streaming across the campaign that reads "Funding Successful," at which point all the contributors' credit cards are collectively swiped. As a backer of many Kickstarter projects, I find I'm more inclined to contribute larger amounts if I know I've got some time to assure I have the funds in my account. Kickstarter appeals to me because it clearly states when and at what time a project's campaign will end. On the other hand, many people like to make a contribution and avoid the surprise of checking their bank statements to discover a $25 transaction for something they don't remember buying two months before; Indiegogo caters to these contributors. Not every backer checks frequently enough on either site just to see how that cool indie film they helped fund is coming along.

Choosing a platform is all about options, and as a crowdfunder, you have to figure out what will be best for your specific film project. If you're trying to make a sci-fi feature for $100,000 that requires stunts and shooting locations, chances are you might be more inclined to try your luck with Kickstarter, since if you only end up raising $2,000 on Indiegogo, there's not a whole lot you'll be able to do with what amounts to 2% of your projected budget. However, if you're making a short film for $5,000 and raise only $3,500, you may still be able to put together a very decent short film, and in this case, Indiegogo would be the right choice.

TOOLS OF THE TRADE

As with anything else, the right tools can get the job done right and with fewer headaches. Therefore, another decisive factor when choosing a crowdfunding platform is finding out what tools each one has at its disposal to make the arduous task of raising funds a bit more bearable. Here are some of the basic tools that both Indiegogo and Kickstarter offer to their users, which are usually located at the top of your campaign's homepage:

- Campaign/Project Home
- Updates
- Comments
- Funders/Backers

The names may differ (Indiegogo calls contributors "funders" whereas Kickstarter calls them "backers"), but the uses are the same. And though these are essentially tabs, I view them more as tools because, if used correctly, they make campaigning much less time-consuming. "Campaign/Project Home" makes it easy to get visitors back to your main page on which your pitch, project description, and perks are located. "Updates" are how crowdfunders can keep contributors in the loop with what's going on with the campaign. Contributors can interact with the campaigners as "Comments," and the "Funders" or "Backers" tabs list the people who've contributed to your project. Here, contributors can control what information to keep private and what to publicize, such as the amount given, in the event a contributor wants to keep the exact amount he or she gave out of the spotlight, or his or her identity, in case someone wants to remain anonymous.

One tool that Indiegogo offers that Kickstarter doesn't is its "Gallery" tab, which I found extremely helpful during my campaign for *Cerise*. Here's an example of some of the things that Sam Platizky, writer, producer, and crowdfunder for *Red Scare*, a zombie farce of 1950s propaganda movies, includes in his gallery:

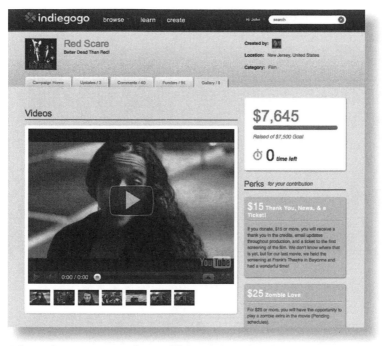

The Red Scare *team's gallery is filled with fun videos for potential contributors to peruse.*

Sam used his Indiegogo gallery primarily for posting video updates about the progress of *Red Scare* and also included the design he ultimately used for his T-shirts perk. But you can use your gallery for plenty of other things, too, from posting pictures and videos to downloadable gifts like desktop patterns, and even PDFs, in case you want to share a page or two of your script with your funders. The gallery can be a very helpful addition to a rigorous campaign and can also serve as a time capsule of your months as a crowdfunder.

SOCIAL MEDIA INTEGRATION

All crowdfunding platforms have what usually proves to be the most important feature in any platform — social media integration. The difference between crowdfunding and traditional fundraising is the fact that if you're choosing a website to host your project, you'll probably be using the Internet as your primary method of bringing in funds, and today that means email and social media. Indiegogo and Kickstarter cover the basic social networking sites, namely Twitter and Facebook, and make it easy for you to share your project with your friends and the rest of the world. Some websites even include LinkedIn and Google Plus as well. Here's an example of Indiegogo's toolbar:

Indiegogo's "Share" toolbar offers an easy way to spread the word about your campaign via email and across various social networks.

The "Share" toolbar, which is usually located directly beneath your pitch video, also includes an "Embed" button and a trackable "shortlink" so you can see how many clicks you get on your link. This can prove highly important for recording metrics about your campaign, which can give you a sense of what may be working and what may not be, numerically speaking, of course.

ANALYTICS

Speaking of numbers, the ability to keep track of what's going on with your campaign behind the scenes can be a very important factor as well, and some crowdfunding platforms do it more effectively than others. With Indiegogo, for instance, once you're signed in and go to "Manage Campaign" and click on "Dashboard," you'll find three tabs: "Analytics," which includes a campaign summary and campaigner stats; "Funds," which keeps track of important information like who's contributing, how they are contributing, and whether or not their funds have been disbursed to the campaigner; and "Fulfillment," which delves into the details of individual funders, how much they've contributed to your campaign, and their email and mailing addresses for delivery of their perks.

Most important here is the analytics tab primarily because it keeps track of some critical information, like how many views your campaign has gotten and how many contributions. It also shows how many of your funders have referred someone else to your Indiegogo page, and even lets you see how much money was brought in by a contributor's referral. For instance, on my page, I know that I referred fourteen people, seven of whom became contributors giving a total of $335 to *Cerise*. Friend and fellow crowdfunder Gary King referred 161 people, and out of that three of them contributed an additional $235. Marinell referred an impressive 222 people, with one of them giving my short film $10.

These are some interesting metrics to keep track of, but keep in mind that they are only accurate if you're making use of the social networking widgets found in the "Share This Campaign" section of your Indiegogo page. I didn't make use of them, because in reality, I didn't just share my film project to fourteen people; I did the bulk of my promotion directly through Facebook, Twitter, and my email. Again, this shows how important it is to make use of the tools your crowdfunding platform provides and learn how to use them to benefit your campaign efforts most.

CUSTOMER SERVICE

If you have any questions, you shouldn't hesitate in contacting the company's customer support, especially if this is your first time crowdfunding. If customer support is an important feature to you, then Indiegogo may be the better platform since it is renowned for its first-rate Customer Happiness Team, whereas Kickstarter lags behind in this arena. In fact, when actor, writer, and filmmaker Gregor Collins finished crowdfunding for his feature-length dramedy *It's a Good Day to Die*, he was so disappointed with Kickstarter's lack of customer service skills that he wrote a letter called "Wake Up, Kickstarter," which appeared on the website Film Courage. In it, Gregor explains to the indie film community that Kickstarter doesn't care about its customers the way, say, Apple does. "At the end of our campaign," his P.S. begins, "we pay you 5% of our hard-fought-for money. So I don't think it's unreasonable to expect at least 5% effort on your part to be genuine."

Today, customer service can also fall into the realm of social networking, and your crowdfunding platform should have an active Twitter and Facebook account and should be doing more than simply promoting its "Project of the Day." If you have a quick question that can be answered in 140 characters, you should be able to ask it to @Indiegogo or @Kickstarter and receive a timely reply. That's what customer happiness is really all about — timeliness and efficiency.

APPEARANCE

Although Aristotle wrote in his classic pamphlet *The Poetics* that spectacle was the least important element of all good theater, when it comes to choosing a crowdfunding platform, appearances can weigh a little heavier on the decision-making process. Today, design is very influential in just about everything, and this is especially true for websites. They must be eye-catching and make a visitor want to stop and stay a while. We've all encountered the eyesore of a website that uses ten different colors, five different fonts, and perhaps has a photo or two stretched and strewn haphazardly about. And then there are those not optimized for mobile devices — the kiss of death in a world that moves at the speed of electricity.

I notice that many of the film projects I give money to choose Kickstarter over Indiegogo, and when I ask for some reasons why, one of them is always appearance. Many times I'll hear that Kickstarter's website is more streamlined than Indiegogo's, complete with a color scheme that is easy on the eye, including the hopeful green of Kickstarter's unique "You're a Backer" stamp. Kickstarter also has a catchier name, playing off of the basic principle that crowdfunding helps filmmakers "kick-start" their projects. RocketHub, another crowdfunding platform, makes use of design on a much grander scale than both its counterparts. It boasts a "Creative Launchpad" motif, in which each image plays an integral part, such as one fuel indicator counting up toward the campaign's goal while another counts down to the campaign's deadline, plus a big red button above them that reads "Fuel This Project."

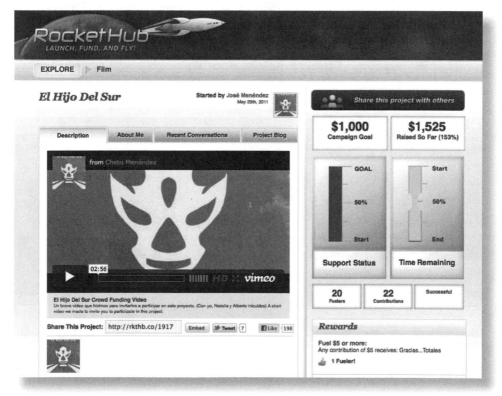

RocketHub's design makes campaigners feel like they're at the helm of a spaceship ready to blast off and discover a new frontier of film funding

We all have different aesthetic biases, so appearance shouldn't be such a major factor in your decision to choose one crowdfunding platform over another. Each of the other points, from "All or Nothing" and "All or More" to the platform's ability to keep track of the metrics behind your campaign, are much more pressing points to consider. You probably won't find a platform that has everything you're looking for, but if you can check off as many of these platform assets as you can, it will no doubt lead to a more productive and enjoyable crowdfunding experience.

These are the basics you need to consider before choosing the right platform for your crowdfunding campaign. If you're planning on raising some pretty substantial funds, you'll find some helpful information in Chapter Thirty-Three, where I delve a bit deeper into the pros and cons of Indiegogo and Kickstarter when it comes to crowdfunding for $30,000 and beyond.

Chapter Nine

...

HOME IN ON
YOUR TARGET AUDIENCE

IN TODAY'S WORLD, anybody who has a halfway decent idea, a modicum of skill with a camera, and a slight sensitivity to the art of storytelling can be a filmmaker. Most often, the film's success has less to do with the quality of the finished product than with the fact that the filmmakers took time to focus on a target audience. Lots of filmmakers settle for wanting to make a movie that everyone will enjoy. But who's *everyone*? With so many different tastes in films out in the world, we traditionally break those tastes up into single-word genres like action, comedy, drama, thriller, and western. But since the inception of these genres, the world has grown vaster, and as a result, those genres have been broken down into smaller categories that include psychological thrillers, bromances, and dramedies, so that we as filmmakers can reach out to even more people.

But it hasn't stopped there. Genres have been broken down into niches, very tightly focused audiences who enjoy certain elements that mainstream movies don't always address. It's all a microcosm within a macrocosm, and it is this smallest cosmos that DIY film-makers should aspire to and find success in on their way up the stairway to the stars. The same way you'll ultimately devise an idea that caters to a particular genre and niche, your crowdfunding campaign should home in on that very specific target audience as well.

That's the basic concept behind crowdfunding — you're not only running a campaign to secure the funds you need to make your film, you're also raising awareness from an audience that wants to see your finished film. You're building a fan base with every dollar that is added toward your crowdfunding goal. Once your film is complete and ready to screen at film festivals, you'll have an army of people in various regions eagerly awaiting it because they may not only enjoy films like yours, but they also may have helped fund yours.

That said, it's very important to figure out who your target audience is *before* you launch your campaign, and that takes a little research to see which niches and communities your film will be most relevant to. Sometimes, this is fairly easy. *Mother's Red Dress* is billed on its Kickstarter page as "a social issue feature film," so of course now we have a better idea of the kinds of people who will watch it, namely, the socially conscious. But even with this very focused niche of "social issues," we have to try and dig even deeper and ask what kind of social issue does the film focus on. A brief read through the description reveals that *Mother's Red Dress* is about "abuse, domestic violence and mental illness," according to Kyra Dawson of the website The Scribe's Desk. But producer and campaigner John Paul Rice also delves deeper in one section of his Kickstarter page he titled "our motivation to tell this story," in which he states the following:

> A tragic love story, the film deals with the effects of domestic violence, abuse and mental illness. The message of the film is that the denial of trauma causes mental dysfunction. We created a film based on the hope that the main character would possibly begin his road to recovery once he faced the truth of his past.

It's very important to get as factored down to your true target audience as possible if you're going to have a smooth and successful campaign and film. Just like the simple phrase "social issue" adds much to this film's niche and genre, so does the phrase "hardcore horror" in the Kickstarter campaign for *Hardcore Indie*, a documentary about the making of two hardcore horror films, *Crawl Bitch Crawl*, directed by Oklahoma Ward, and *Screen*, directed by David Paul Baker. Sometimes a niche or two can be in the title of your film, as in *Ninjas vs*

Monsters, directed by Justin Timpane, which will no doubt appeal to people who enjoy a good martial arts film as well as those who like monster movies.

The real work about homing in on a target audience is figuring out where to find that audience by asking yourself two questions: Who will watch my movie? Who might help me promote my film and my crowdfunding campaign? Luckily, the Internet makes both of these tasks a little less intimidating, and with a few hours researching keyword results on Google, you'll swiftly work your way from the outer rings to the bull's-eye.

WEBSITES AND BLOGS

Websites are probably the first place you should start to seek out your target audience and immerse yourself in that genre or niche. I subscribe to the belief that it's always best to start big and work your way down. So if I were making a zombie film, for instance, the first online venues I'd sign up for would be the biggies like Fangoria. But a quick Google search of "zombie websites" reveals two great resources — The Zombie Network and ZombieSquad. A refined search of "zombie movie websites" adds a few more to the list, and a further refined search of "zombie comedies" gives us an abundance of resources that tell us the "Top Ten Zombie Comedies," but also affords us the names of websites where we can start conversations with other like-minded zombie-lovers. Ultimately, after working your way into this particular community, you can gradually men-tion your zombie comedy and eventually you'll have a following of people who will be excited to see your film, but more importantly, you may have a newfound network of people who'll help you with its funding and promotion. Hence, your army begins to seed.

Blog sites are another powerful resource at your disposal to help you zero in on your target audience. If you're making a bromance, you'll find tons of blogs maintained by people who enjoy a good, solid story about guys being guys like *The Hangover*. After searching "bromance," two solid blogs that top off a long list of other blog sites, websites, and Facebook pages are A Bromance Appreciation Blog and Bromance.

FACEBOOK SEARCHES

Okay, back to zombies for a moment. A quick search on Facebook, arguably one of the most innovative ways of socializing the world has ever seen, gives me a list of pages with the word "zombie" in it, one of which has almost 96,000 "Likes." By clicking the "Like" button and posting a link to your crowdfunding campaign here, there's a fairly good chance that the more hardcore zombie fans out of that 96,000 will see it, and out of that, there's no telling how many of them might actually contribute to your campaign or "Share" it with their friends on Facebook. The potential is there, and it's huge. It's just a matter of setting up a derrick and tapping into this fertile landscape and there's no doubt some funds will flow.

TWITTER SEARCHES

Equally as important as Facebook, blog, and web searches in discovering and maximizing your target audience are Twitter searches. You can discover an entire world of potential contributors and supporters for your crowdfunding campaign and build it up into a powerful audience. When I started raising funds for *Cerise*, I only had a couple hundred Twitter followers, and within the course of two months of hardcore campaigning, that number doubled. Now, I have over 1,800 followers. When you indulge in conversations with the people you follow and participate in Twitter groups like #FilmIn140, a weekly discussion about movies, or the very popular #Scriptchat, by the end of that hour or so of chatting, you'll usually end up with three to five new followers each week. Your main concern should be tapping into not only filmcentric groups, but also those that relate to the genre and niches of your film.

Get On Your Platform's Homepage

Yes, it's true — there are people out there who frequent Indiegogo, Kickstarter, and other crowdfunding platforms in search of interesting projects that they can help toward their goals. But they won't find your film project unless you make it easy for them, and it doesn't get any easier than by landing your film's campaign on your platform's homepage, like ferret-friendly filmmaker Alison Parker did with her project *The Ferret Squad*.

The way to attract the most attention to your campaign is to be featured on your platform's home page.

Each platform has its own criteria regarding how campaigns get to become featured projects on the website's homepage. Indiegogo, for instance, has something called the "gogofactor," an algorithm that measures a campaign's activity. If your gogofactor is high and steady, you'll eventually be rewarded for all your hard work and dedication to your campaign by being featured on the Indiegogo homepage. You may even get a mention in their monthly newsletter that goes out to all their customers, which can further expand your reach to individuals who've funded other projects on Indiegogo before and are looking to come on board as Associate Producer for the next big film project.

I often mention at seminars and panel discussions the impressive fact that 70% of the funds that came in during my campaign for *Cerise* were from strangers, and people's eyebrows perk up immediately. I attribute this to *Cerise's* becoming a featured project on Indiegogo fairly quickly because of its intense level of activity. As a result, I attracted the attention of many wonderful people like Ryan Ronning, Ben Gerber, and especially Gavin Ap'Morrygan, who's not only helped *Cerise* immensely, but is now a major force in helping out projects all across the indie film community. So by keeping your activity up and showing that you are a crowdfunding force to be reckoned with, you'll be given more opportunities to demonstrate that drive and passion, and people will see it, and you will be rewarded for it.

Chapter Ten

. . .

CREATE (AND MAINTAIN)
YOUR CAMPAIGN STRATEGY

ONCE YOU'VE ESTABLISHED the target audience for your film as well as for your crowdfunding campaign — from the overall genre down to the most exact niche — it's time to figure out how to reach that audience. And once you reach the audience, the next and more important part becomes how to keep them engaged and checking in on your project's status long after your campaign has ended. The ultimate question, however, is how do you keep your film project on peoples' minds without becoming a total nuisance?

It is therefore highly important to not dive into your crowdfunding campaign blindfolded. Too often, people go in with the attitude that they're just going to "try it out and see if it actually works," and yes, I was guilty of this, too. The fact is that it does work: as of April, 2012, Kickstarter helped to raise $119.6 million in funding for its successful projects over the course of three years, and in that same month, President Obama signed into law the JOBS (Jump-start Our Business Startups) Act, which makes equity investment possible through crowdfunding (read more about this in Chapter Thirty-Four). This development was preceded by the President joining forces with Indiegogo for his Startup America Partnership offering small businesses and entrepreneurs the chance to raise up to $30 million in startup funding.

Whether it'll work for you depends on whether you "do [it] or do not," because, as Jedi Master Yoda dictates, "there is no try." The worst-case scenario is that if you only "try it out" and fail, you've hopefully learned a lot from the experience, but it will be at the expense of having lost some credibility with the people who may have already funded you and your project, which means you'll have to spend your time searching for a whole new core of supporters and contributors for your next crowdfunding attempt. So, if you're going to crowdfund, do it for real, with the intention of taking home well over your initial fundraising goal. To do this, you have to have a strategy in mind.

When you watch TV commercials like the ones from Geico and Progressive, each commercial seems to build off of the next, and that is part of the marketing strategy for these car insurance companies. Someone planned this out long before Geico launched the first of its "It's so easy, a caveman could do it" campaign. Similarly, your entire crowdfunding campaign, like any solid, compelling story, should have a beginning, middle, and end. Traditionally in fundraising, this could be seen as the *launch*, *run*, and *fulfillment*. The forward direction of a film should be set up during the first act, its beginning, and so should your campaign, so that when you launch, it will start off strong and grab the attention of your target audience. It's the pivotal second act, however, that can make or break the film experience for its viewers, so the second act of your campaign, the one- to three-month run itself, should be soundly spliced together and unveil new and interesting things at every twist and turn. The majority of those twists and turns should be set up before the launch. By the end of a film, an audience wants fulfillment, so by the conclusion of your campaign, your contributors should feel just as fulfilled when they receive their perks in a timely manner.

Much of your campaign's strategy should revolve around the central themes or concepts that are present in your film. While you can run a campaign in a more straightforward manner, offering standard perks like executive and associate producer credit and T-shirts, it probably won't be much fun for you to run. More importantly, it may start to feel a bit flat to potential contributors. As crowdfunders, we should go the distance with our campaigns in the same way we would as filmmakers making our movies because people will undoubtedly see the effort that is poured into a project or campaign and appreciate it even more, which could mean the difference between receiving a $10 contribution and a $50 one.

When strategizing your campaign, think about the important themes and motifs that are running through it. Once you've got those elements solidified, think about how you can bring those elements into your campaign. For instance, *Cerise* is a movie about how something from one's past can keep him or her from realizing his or her full potential. How did I work that concept into my crowdfunding campaign? Easy: I didn't. It's too grandiose an idea, not to mention very abstract. But *Cerise* also revolves around the fact that the protagonist is a spelling bee champ who lost because of a single word. So, I took the idea of a spelling bee and incorporated it into every element of my campaign, from my pitch video down to the descriptions of my perks. Even the lowest level perk was centered on words, which still falls into the wide realm of a spelling bee.

Another example is the short film *Sync* by Brendon Fogle, which is about the relationship between a grandfather and his grandson and the connection they find through disconnection. The film revolves around the concept of nostalgia, specifically in the form of vinyl records. Brendon's campaign follows suit and reflects that concept, primarily in his perks and update videos.

Of course, there is also the element of surprise, or spontaneity, and those things can't be planned out in too much detail or too far in advance. For instance, midway through your campaign you may want to add a new perk limited to a certain number, which is an excellent idea and can really reinvigorate your campaign. It should, however, still fit in some way with what you've already established as your campaign scheme. Some of these things can be planned out and incorporated into your perks, as well. The fine folks behind the feature-length film *Tilt* incorporated their backers into "*Tilt* the

Town," which started out as a simple biography but morphed into something more immense than any of the campaign's 223 backers could have expected. What seemed to grow and prosper organically was partially planned out in some detail during the initial stages of their campaign, but it was also allowed to flourish into something much greater. (Don't worry, we'll examine the basic concept of *Tilt the Town* in the "Crowd Studies" section of this book.)

Maintaining your campaign is an important aspect of any crowd-funding endeavor, especially sustaining interest in it after you've reached your goal. Remember, the campaign's not finished just because you raised the money and made your film. You've got contributors who are awaiting perks and who are probably eager to see the finished product because, naturally, they're curious as to what their money went to. It's also important to keep the same tone and demeanor you established at the beginning of your campaign right up until the end, since it will show your supporters that you are an organized person who knows the value of structure. More so, it'll show that you are fully focused on your film project and its campaign, which helped bring the finished film one step closer to excellence.

Chapter Eleven

• • •

GIVE YOURSELF ENOUGH TIME

I'VE SEEN CAMPAIGNS raise upward of $5,000 in as little as two months like *Cerise* did, and I've seen other campaigns like Lucas McNelly's *A Year Without Rent* reach 75% of its total in the final few days and hours. However, you shouldn't rely on stories like Lucas's to make you feel you can do the same in a month or even a few days of crowdfunding. Time is a delicate matter, and it varies for each individual project. That said, you should take some time to decide on how much time you'll realistically need to raise the funds you're after. Most crowdfunding platforms have parameters regarding how long a campaign can be active. Kickstarter, for instance, allows either thirty or sixty days to run a campaign; with Indiegogo, a campaign can last anywhere from a few weeks to three months. But as Indiegogo's metrics suggest, more time does not always lead to more money. For *Cerise's* campaign, I chose ninety days because I thought that'd be a safe number, and through nonstop campaigning, my team and I were able to hit our $5,000 goal in two months.

That said, deciding how much time you're going to need to successfully crowdfund your film project depends on a few factors, the first and most important being how much money you are hoping to raise. Lower amounts from a few hundred to a few thousand dollars will probably not need as much time as, say, a goal of $20,000 for a feature-length movie. But even this first factor depends heavily on two other factors: how large your current network is and how much of your own time you have to invest in campaigning.

Size matters, so the scope of your current network will play an integral role as you determine how long your campaign should run for. I use the word "current" because once you start crowdfunding, your network will undoubtedly grow, especially by sharing your project across your social networks. If you've only started Tweeting or finally created a Facebook page because "everyone else has one" and you've only got a handful of friends and followers, then raising substantial funds may be a bit more difficult. Not impossible, but more challenging than if you waited a few months to a year to build up not only your network but your credibility as a filmmaker and then launch your campaign when you've got a bit more clout or, at the very least, more than only your close friends following you on Twitter.

While a larger network will ultimately aid you toward a successful campaign that much quicker, that success also walks hand in hand with how much time you have at your disposal to put into your campaign. Here I'll say it again: *Crowdfunding is a full-time job*. If you've already got a full-time job that's paying your bills and leaves hardly any time to eat and sleep, let alone maintain an active crowdfunding campaign, then raising $50,000 will be that much more difficult. Again, it's not impossible, but it will be more arduous than if you were working part-time at the neighborhood coffee shop and spending your downtime interacting with your network promoting your film campaign.

A successful campaign is one that doesn't sleep, but it also doesn't spend all of its time talking about itself; aside from mentioning your campaign a few times a day on the social sites and sending out an email blast once every few days, you also have to mingle with your potential contributors on a more personal level. This is where all that time comes into play, but that's also where your team comes in to help. In terms of how much time you have available to invest in your campaign, you can take solace in the fact that there is no "I" in "team" — everyone on your team should participate and split the time it takes to keep active, both in crowdfunding and socializing. One thing to be aware of is that no one will give it the same 100% as you will give it, since, after all, it is *your* project and not theirs. However much time and effort is given to your campaign, rest assured that every bit will help to spread the word and bring in that funding.

Crowdfunding isn't a race to some imaginary finish line, so give yourself enough time, and, based on your answers to the questions of how large your current network is and how much time you have to invest in campaigning, you should be able to choose a time frame that will best suit your individual campaign needs. Some solid data to keep in mind is this: According to Indiegogo, "campaigns that set a funding deadline between 60 and 70 days raise, on average, 141% more money than their shorter or longer campaign counterparts." Compare that with Kickstarter's sixty-day cap on its campaigns, and it can only mean there is much truth to this statement.

With all these basics covered and your "Way" plotted out before, it's time to delve into the actual running of your crowdfunding campaign. There is, however, a certain way of going to the crowd for help financing your film, and that's where *Crowdfunding for Filmmakers* really comes into play. The next section will open up before you a pathway that you can follow to a successful campaign, so that you will be able to make that film you keep playing in your head without worrying whether you can actually afford to make it. So let's begin to learn the Way to a successful film campaign.

· PART TWO ·
SUMMARY POINTS

- Go with the *Tao* (the Way) of traditional fundraising; the tools of the trade are the only difference between that and crowdfunding.

- The more skilled your teammates are, the smoother your campaign will run.

- Many factors should be considered when deciding which crowdfunding platform you should run your campaign on, such as "All or Nothing" or "All or More" deadlines, the right tools, social media integration, analytics, and appearance.

- The size of your current network will play an important role in deciding how long your campaign should run and how much money you should raise.

- Plan your campaign out as a strategy, leaving some room for spontaneity.

· PART TWO ·
EXERCISES

1. What is the logline of your film? Be succinct (short and on point). Is it a short film? A feature-length film? Based on this, how much money, at minimum, do you think you'll need to bring this film from script to screen? Write it down.

2. Think about the audience of the film you want to crowdfund for. What genre best fits the logline you wrote for it? What niche(s) does your film fit into best? Is it made for a particular demographic? Basically, who are the people who are going to want to see your film once it's made?

3. If you don't already have one, set up a Twitter account. Start following film people (filmmakers, screenwriters, bloggers, and production companies), which can be found through a keyword search. Then, start *interacting* with them, as well as Tweeting interesting, relevant things to ensure the #followback.

PART 3 CAMPAIGN PERSONALIZATION

Chapter Twelve

...

TE: INTEGRITY IS THE TAO TO (KA-) CHING!

WHOLENESS. INDIVISIBILITY. UNIFICATION. These are all words that describe the Taoist principle of *Te*, which literally translates to "integrity," or moral uprightness. When someone has a strong sense of moral principle, he or she knows something solid about him- or herself, and usually that something can't be compromised. How might this apply to crowdfunding for an indie film? In a single word: *personalization*.

One reason for the success of *Cerise* and many other crowdfunding campaigns like it is that it was geared with one principle in mind: make everything about your audience. The movie itself is the filmmaker's creation, and it's his or her passion that fuels the drive to launch and navigate a campaign to raise the funds to make it. It would be wonderful if all the people who contributed to your campaign did so simply to help an aspiring filmmaker soar to the top of his or her dreams and start a career in the entertainment industry, but that's not always the case. Many times, people contribute to a campaign because of what they will receive in return, and we as crowdfunders should be sensitive to this fact.

This is where the principle of *Te* can fit into various aspects of your campaign. The first and most important lesson it teaches us is humility, helping us realize that our campaigns are only partially about us and mostly about our potential contributors. We may have learned from TV commercials peddling products ranging from powerful gardening tools to OxiClean that selling something simply doesn't always work. Crowdfunding is not selling, although you are selling yourself to a certain extent and must therefore give some of yourself to your campaign and your contributors. Of course, campaigns can be run in a very OxiClean fashion and still be successful, but where's the fun and creativity in that? More importantly, where's the connection between crowdfunder and contributor?

Integrity is a trait in people that is best shown, not told, and the way to showcase your *Tê* during your crowdfunding campaign is to put some of yourself in every aspect of your campaign, from your pitch and perks to your promotion. This is where personalization comes into play. By going that extra mile and showing your potential contributors the real person behind your campaign, you become the very definition of integrity, a real mensch, and open yourself and your film to a brave new world of possibilities far exceeding the limits of the amount of money you'll ultimately raise.

Chapter Thirteen

• • •

YOUR PITCH VIDEO:
MAKE IT ABOUT YOUR PROJECT
AND YOURSELF

FIRST IMPRESSIONS ARE EVERYTHING. That's why the most important aspect of your crowdfunding campaign is your pitch video, which is essentially an elevator pitch in the form of a short video. It will be the first thing anyone sees after typing your campaign's URL into a browser. Before we delve into what a personalized pitch is, it's important we take a quick look at a trio of things that are *not* pitches:

- A photograph, no matter how expertly shot
- Your film's trailer
- Backstage and/or interview footage

Although the cliché is true, that a picture speaks a thousand words, the chances that it'll speak those words loudly enough to get some-one to part with a hard-earned $20 bill are slim. The trailer for your film is a sales tool geared to get people to want to see your film, not a pitch tool, which exists to convince them to come aboard and help get it made. And as humorous and insightful as backstage and inter-view footage can be, rarely will it make anyone want to contribute to your film's campaign, especially if you're staring off at a twenty-degree angle toward an imaginary interviewer talking about how awesome your film is going to be.

When I pieced together my pitch video for *Cerise*, I wasn't exactly sure how to go about it. I did some research, of course, and watched a lot of pitch videos, many of which, quite honestly, didn't impress me. Some were interesting, and they all spoke to me, the viewer, about a particular project and how integral my support would be to getting it made, but the majority of them didn't make me want to plug in my debit card digits and join the cause. I wanted to try something different with my pitch video, so I got together with Marinell and Alain and shot some footage, which I then edited the following week and uploaded the pitch onto YouTube. I launched the campaign, but before I sent out my first Tweet, I became hesitant, besieged by doubts and questions: Who's gonna want to help me make my film? Is this pitch video any good? Why am I even doing this?

As I was about to click the delete button and go make *Cerise* the way I'd made my other seven films, with my own money, I saw on Twitter that Indiegogo had mentioned me in a Tweet beckoning its followers to check out the Project of the Day, *Cerise*, with its "awesome pitch clip." It seems my video had a fan who had taken it upon him- or herself to start the promotion for me while I was basking in the cold shadow of doubt and fear of failure. That's when I realized just how much potential my pitch video's fun nature and personal touch could have in crowdfunding my first film.

This scene from Cerise's pitch video shows potential funders just how much love we'd express to an Associate Producer.

Essentially, your pitch video is the one and only chance you have to really sell *yourself*, not necessarily your project. Take some time to talk to your potential contributors. Tell them about yourself, and then tell them why you want to make this film and why they should help make it happen. Again, keep in mind the "they" of this whole enterprise. We may think crowdfunding is about us, but the word "I" is only a small letter in the word; the bulk of it is all "crowd," so make it about the crowd.

A personalized pitch video like the one for *Cerise* and many other successful campaigns can be broken into three key parts: the *introduction*, the *pitch*, and the *showcase*. The introduction is your opportunity to make the acquaintance of your potential contributors and let them know a little about who you are not only as a filmmaker, but as a person, too. It's your chance to quickly make a connection with your future contributors. My introduction consisted of letting people know the three most important things about me: I'm a poet, filmmaker, and adjunct professor. Your introduction should be as short and on-point as you can get it.

Once you conclude your introduction, it's time to turn your attention to your actual pitch, which can also be broken into three parts: the *précis*, *purpose*, and *perks*. The shortest form of a précis, or summary, in filmmaking is the logline, which is traditionally kept at one or two sentences that encapsulate the bulk of what your story is about. Think of it as a brief introduction to your project. This is followed by the purpose, where you can quickly tell your potential contributors why you're raising funds for your film through crowdfunding, what those funds will be used for, and any other pertinent information about the reason for this campaign. After that, it's usually a good idea to briefly mention some of the perks that people will get in exchange for their monetary contribution to your film project. Granted, I went the extra yard with my pitch video for *Cerise* and shot short scenes to illustrate the perks at each of my perk levels, but not all pitch videos have to be this detailed.

A mistake that many crowdfunders make is not being in their pitch videos. The truth is you *must* appear in your pitch video. As I mentioned earlier, there are not too many people out there who will give money to a photograph or a movie trailer, let alone to a ghost, and that's what you become to potential contributors when you don't appear in your own video. People give to people, and while it's true that no one likes to ask others for money, by choosing to crowdfund, that's exactly what you're doing, and the least you can do for these individuals is ask them as personally as possible. In this case, your pitch video is as personal as it's going to get.

An excellent example of a simpler pitch video that worked wonders is the one for filmmaker Jeanie Finlay's *Sound It Out*, a documentary about the last record shop in Teesside, UK. I'd originally made her acquaintance when she asked if I'd give her some feedback on her Indiegogo campaign. I watched her pitch video, which was really just a trailer for the film. I told her she needed to be in the video and ask people for money directly rather than having them read her written pitch below the trailer. She decided to keep it as is and launched her campaign to raise the funds needed to finish *Sound It Out*.

A few weeks later, I received a Tweet from Jeanie with a link. It seems she had not been raising very much money during the opening weeks of her campaign, so she reconsidered my advice and recorded a new pitch video, this time with her in it. Practically overnight she saw a substantial difference. Funds started rolling in through tons of promotion on her part, and when all was said and done, she'd overshot her initial goal of $3,000 by $1,468! Now *Sound It Out* has screened at film festivals all over the world, including well-known festivals Sheffield Doc Fest, Silverdocs, and Edinburgh International Film Festival.

That's Jeanie Finlay starring in her pitch video for her feature-length documentary Sound It Out.

Jeanie then recorded another pitch video with her once again taking center stage when she launched a second successful Indiegogo campaign for $5,000 to get her and her team to the highly prestigious SXSW Film Festival, where *Sound It Out* had its world premiere. And after that, Jeanie went on to record a third pitch video to bring *Sound It Out* to theaters across the United Kingdom. This time, she partnered with Sheffield Doc Fest and brought in $828 over her $10,000 goal. That's over $20,000 in crowdfunding between three campaigns with three very personal pitch videos at the forefront of Jeanie's multiple successes.

The final part of a personalized pitch is the showcase, in which you build your credibility as a filmmaker by showing samples of your prior film work and highlighting any awards or recognition you or your work may have received. You've already built up the *Tē* necessary to get viewers of your pitch video to listen to you through your introduction and pitch, but now you need to show them you know your way around a camera and film set. In my pitch video for *Cerise*, I showcased a few shots from some of the films I'm most proud of, as well as a sitcom pilot I directed which won two awards for excellence in filmmaking. What better way to build up your potential contributors' confidence in your current film project than with some film festival recognition for your prior work?

One thing to keep in mind is time. Even though we're living in a world where most people are more oriented to visual images over words, attention spans are rapidly diminishing. A pitch video, therefore, should be as short as possible, and I would suggest a runtime between two and three minutes at most. Anything longer, such as synopses, director's statements, and other stories about what inspired the film, can be added to the "About" section beneath your pitch video. Your perks will be listed in greater detail to the right of your pitch video, keeping the pitch video itself as an introduction to you, your project, and what you can do, so long as you can convince those watching it to become contributors to your next great masterpiece.

Chapter Fourteen

...

PERKS: MAKE THEM
ABOUT YOUR PROJECT AND
YOUR CONTRIBUTORS

THE REAL MUSCLES behind crowdfunding are the perks and the fundamental concept that if you give me money, you get something in return. While there's nothing wrong with offering the more typical perks like T-shirts, DVD copies of the finished film, signed posters, pages from the script, and associate and executive producer credit in your film, it's much better to think outside the money box and get personal with your perks. Of course, once you find out what that actually means and how time-consuming being personal can be, you'll understand why a lot of campaigners stick to the basics, especially in the midst of a day job, family obligations, house chores, and just having a social life.

At the end of the day, however, it's important to keep a couple of things in mind. First, the film you're crowdfunding for probably won't be the last film you ever make, which means you'll need money for future projects, and crowdfunding will certainly be an option, especially in the wake of the JOBS Act (see Chapter Thirty-Four). Second, you're not only crowdfunding for funds, but for a crowd as well, and by keeping a person-to-person connection with your contributors, they will be more likely to contribute to another of your campaigns in the future. So the question to ask yourself really isn't how much you want to make this particular film, but how much you want to be a filmmaker.

Even I fell into the standard definition world of perk offerings. Many of *Cerise's* perks are pretty traditional. At the $50 level, I'm offering a T-shirt that says, "I spelt *Cerise*," plus a signed copy of the DVD. At $100, contributors can visit the set as an associate producer and enjoy a classic Jersey meal on me at a local diner, which is border-line personal since I offer a small bit of myself, with my background being Greek and New Jersey being the diner capital of the world. And at $500, contributors not only get awarded the title of executive producer, but they also receive an invitation to a private screening of *Cerise* in New York City.

What you'll notice here is that the perks don't have to be 100% personalized, but if there's just one portion of your perks that offers your contributors a little insight into you as a person and film-maker, then the perk becomes that much more special and has value added to it. Everyone knows a simple DVD isn't worth $50, but a DVD signed by the writer/director of the film and a T-shirt that tells others you supported a cool indie film project are a steal in exchange for a Ulysses S. Grant.

Another example is the short film *Sync*, which I won't delve too deeply into here since Brendon Fogle's short film campaign is one of five I'll be describing in detail in the "Crowd Studies" section. I will say that, like *Cerise*, the campaign for *Sync* may seem at first glance very conventional, but then you'll notice plenty of personalization in his $33 perk, in which he hand-picks a record from his personal collection and mails it to you. For an audiophile like Brendon, he's definitely giving a little of himself to every contributor. At his $78 perk level, he's designing an album cover using a funder's photo so that it looks like an old "Blue Note" album cover from the 1960s. Hip, snazzy, relevant, and definitely personal.

Goodbye Promise, an exploratory feature-length film by writer/director David Branin, is one more example of ordinary perks with a bit of the extraordinary mixed in to add some flavor and spice, and David's $250 perk does exactly that. By contributing at this level to David's Kick-starter campaign, a backer receives not only a personal thank you on

Film Courage, the radio show David hosts with his wife, actress Karen Worden, and a video message from either David or *Goodbye Promise's* lead actor Gregor Collins, but he or she also receives one of David's "delicious and dangerous" homemade apple pies. That's two hours of David's time piecing together an apple pie just for you. It doesn't get much more personal than that. And although he mentions that this particular perk is "specific to those in Los Angeles," it attracted the attention of international indie film supporter Marcella Selbach, who not only funded *Goodbye Promise* at the $250 level, but also flew out to LA for a taste of this magnificently personal perk.

Gregor Collins has gone from actor to writer on an assisted suicide comedy he successfully crowdfunded $15,536 for called *It's a Good Day to Die*, and he borrowed from the success of David's *Goodbye Promise* apple pie perk by offering a package of Cloris Leachman's Delicious Homemade Tortilla Soup, which "turns soup haters into soup lovers." This personalized part of the $100 perk was limited to the first ten Kickstarter backers, but it still breaks up the list of usual suspects by adding a bit of flavor to the mix.

Personalization doesn't just mean offering perks that give your contributors a piece of you or a glimpse into your world. It can also be as simple as being yourself. One of the easiest ways to do this is to focus on wording your perk descriptions in the most unique way possible. Take, for example, the Kickstarter campaign for *This Is Ours*, a feature-length film by Kris and Lindy Boustedt about a couple on the verge of divorce who head to their summer house one last time, where they encounter a pair of free spirits who embody the tradition of the great American landscape. Right at the top of their perk list? For $1, they'll not only give you a thank you on the *This Is Ours* Facebook page (ordinary), but they'll also shout your name from their front porch in the middle of the day (extraordinary). That shows how much they appreciate a contribution, and it shows humility and humor about contributing even a single dollar to their campaign for the finishing funds to complete *This is Ours*.

Your perks should also be as relevant to your film project as possible. Nothing in this world is done haphazardly or by accident; a campaign takes careful strategizing, so when planning out your contributor perks, figure out how you can maximize the connections you make between your actual film and the perks you're offering during your campaign. Take Meg Pinsonneault's feature-length documentary *Gwapa* (*Beautiful*), which documents a Filipino mother's struggle to help get corrective surgery for her three children with facial deformities. It offers as a $50 perk a handcrafted souvenir from Pitogo Island. The film is shot in the Philippines, so this substantial perk represents a solid connection between perk and place.

The bottom line is to make your perks about your contributors. Think about the most beloved holidays in the US, like Christmas, Valentine's Day, and Easter. As much as we'd like to think they're all about giving, they're really not. People like to receive things. Yes, some people do contribute without much care about what they'll get in return, but these altruistic Bruce Wayne types come around once in a dark night. You will ultimately receive a Tweet or email from a contributor asking where that T-shirt he paid for is or when she'll get the DVD she spent $50 on. This is all fine and normal. Crowdfunding is about the crowd, after all.

You've got to be the one who makes a contributor want to up his or her contribution from $10 to $50, and that lies in the personalization of your perks. It happened to me when I funded *Sync*. I knew I wanted to contribute to Brendon's campaign, but I was a bit strapped for cash at the time, and I'd resolved to go for the $12 perk, which included a neat *Sync* sticker. Then I saw the perk directly below it — a record from Brendon's personal collection — and I thought it was very generous of him to offer someone one of his own LPs. Needless to say, I'm very happy with my vinyl copy of Sammy Davis Jr.'s *Greatest Hits*, which Brendon picked out just for me. $33 well spent for a perk well played.

···

PROMOTION: MAKE IT
YOUR WHOLE WORLD
(AND EVERYONE ELSE'S, TOO!)

WHEN I WAS A SENIOR in high school, I took a class called Mass Media, and the teacher spent a great deal of time making us read a textbook about persuasion and various other methods the media use to create a need in people. Not much of it sank in until our teacher started demonstrating these principles by having us analyze TV commercials. He would help us to see how particular commercials used psychology to make us believe that we need to only use Tide if we cared about our family's clean, fresh clothing, or to choose Wheaties over other cereals because our favorite sports player chooses this brand over Frosted Flakes.

As with just about anything else in the world, marketing can make or break a great new product. Today, marketing and advertising are at their most creative, and this will only expand further until the line blurs so much that creativity and marketing become one and the same. Of course, there's a great deal of psychology at work in every advertisement we see. Catchy phrases like "Roll that beautiful bean footage" from the old Bush's Baked Beans commercials are being replaced with higher concept videos that have more depth. Take Chevrolet's "Chevy Runs Deep" campaign, in which sepia-toned photographs of classic cars and trucks are placed in front of landscapes matching the ones in the old photographs, but instead of classic Chevrolets, there are modern ones driving around in full color. A slogan fades in beneath the iconic Chevrolet logo: "Chevy Runs Deep."

Chevrolet is trying to sell you something more than a Volt or Blazer. This particular campaign attempts to sell you the *tradition* behind Chevrolet automobiles. Today more than ever, people don't just want to buy a car, they want to buy into a legacy. Author Michael Margolis demonstrates this concept best in his book *Believe Me*, in which he writes about the notebook company Moleskine. Not many writers would pay $10 plus tax for a standard black hardcover journal when they can get a $2 softcover one with more pages at the neighborhood supermarket. There's really nothing all that special about Moleskine *except* its tradition of being the "legendary notebooks of van Gogh, Matisse and Hemingway." That's what we're buying into when writers buy a Moleskine journal or Cahier. It's not just a notebook, it's a legend.

MARKET YOUR PROJECT AND YOURSELF

How does all this relate to crowdfunding for your latest film project? The same tactics employed in marketing a product should be employed to raise awareness about your crowdfunding campaign. It should keep up with the trends of the time, and in this case, it's all about personalization. You're not simply spreading the word about your film campaign, you're putting yourself out there as well, and therefore, it's important to market yourself with your campaign because, by default, you make your campaign more personal that way.

Sometimes, contributors will support a campaign solely because they like the person behind it; either they know this person or they get a positive vibe from him or her based on the project's pitch video. The quality of the project may not even matter at that point because the crowdfunder has sold him- or herself as filmmaker on this particular project, making it mean something to his or her contributors. In other instances, contributors support projects because they're high concept, they look humorous or interesting, or they revolve around subjects that are long overdue for big and small screens alike. Whatever reasons contributors have for backing your film campaign, it's up to you to convince them it's a worthwhile project to put their money behind.

Rock It Around the Clock

It's no secret that a successful crowdfunding campaign demands around-the-clock promotion. We sometimes get tired of seeing the same commercial repeatedly, but at the end of your prime-time entertainment, you remember that commercial whether you want to or not, unless you changed the channel. In today's technocracy, this translates to constant Tweets, relentless Facebook status updates, email blasts, sleep strikes, the occasional hunger strike, and any other means by which to keep your film campaign on the minds of your friends, family, supporters, contributors, and potential contributors.

This also means not being afraid to have a lot of fun with your promotional tactics and keeping your audience engaged with things like contests, giveaways, and fun videos. Brendon sure had fun with his video updates for *Sync*, which mimicked old 1960s-style TV commercials in which his alter ego, Vance Connors, stands before a turquoise background talking about the various perks. (More on that in my crowd study of *Sync*.)

It's really promotion that makes crowdfunding a full-time job. There's one surefire way to make your campaign a *fool*-time job, and that is to do little or no promotion whatsoever. Those who enter the mysterious realm of crowdfunding with no idea how it works and no drive to research this approach to raising money tend to believe in the false myth that potential funders actively scavenge the Internet searching for projects to throw bundles of cash at. This is similar to believing in the money tree we all have growing in the back of our apartments, hoping we'll be able to harvest enough green to help grow our next film.

A static campaign will undoubtedly end on the same number it started out with, and that's zero. Shakespeare expressed it best in the words of King Lear: "Nothing will come from nothing." No updates, no comments, and no promotion will ultimately result in no money for your film project and a bad taste in your mouth about crowdfunding that wouldn't be there had you done it right from your launch. You have to work hard to get what you want. If you want this money, you should be showing people your desire in every way you can. You need to be honest and proactive, and only then will you find an audience who cares about you and your project enough to help you make it happen.

THERE WILL BE REJECTION

I'm sure many beginning crowdfunders are concerned about the rejection that could result from a film campaign with a strong Internet and social media presence. No one likes to wake up one morning to the realization that yesterday he or she had 205 friends on Facebook and this morning that number is down to 200. But as Twitter and Facebook gain credibility as marketing and advertising tools for companies, so will it be the case amongst various communities of artists. I've already grown accustomed to seeing five to ten different film campaigns being promoted by my friends and followers all along this brave new social landscape.

But yes, if you overdo your promotion and cross the line into spam territory, you will undoubtedly lose friends and followers and will be asked by some people on your email list to remove them from further emails. Or you could attract even more people, as was the case with my campaign for *Cerise*. It all depends on how you handle your promotion and whether you maintain a strategy to keep it all in proper balance, but we'll discuss more of that in Chapters Twenty-Seven and Twenty-Eight.

Promote Yourself *and* Others?

When I crowdfunded for *Cerise*, I was online practically all day long except when I had to sleep, and even that was at a minimum. Everyone knew that I was crowdfunding for my short film, and many of my first funders weren't family members or friends, but other filmmakers, some of whom were crowdfunding for their own film projects at the same time. This confused me at first, my initial thought being *why are these friends and followers contributing to my short film when they're trying to raise money for their feature-length films?* It would make much more sense to put one's own money into his or her own campaign and not give $25 to this campaign and $10 to that, since that's $35 that could help bump that person's campaign total closer toward its crowdfunding goal.

After some thought, it became clear to me that this indie film community that I'd gotten involved with was indeed a community in the truest sense. Everyone was there to help everyone else one way or another. Many times, this meant contributing to *Cerise*, but those who couldn't contribute financially to my short film campaign helped out by spreading the word about *Cerise* to their networks, and from some of those networks financial support flowed in. When something as organic as this happens, you should pay back the people responsible for it, and one way to do this is with a contribution to their projects.

During the *Cerise* campaign, I wasn't able to contribute to any projects since funds were tight, but I made sure to Tweet about projects being run by contributors to my film. Also, Alain and Marinell put in some money to a few projects launched by those who contributed to *Cerise*. Once crowdfunding for my film had ceased, I started pitching in and helping crowdfunders like Gary King, Mattson Tomlin, David Branin, and other filmmakers who had become vital forces of support to my filmmaking endeavors. That said, it's important to give back what you can during your crowdfunding campaign and not only spend lots of time supporting your own project, but also promoting and supporting the film projects of others and strengthening that sense of community that is oftentimes lacking in more mainstream moviemaking.

By combining intense yet distinctive promotional tactics with unique perks and a pitch, you'll have yourself a winning triumvirate. These three Ps of crowdfunding rely heavily on the most important P — personalization, which is perhaps the greatest difference between all the more traditional ways of funding a film and crowdfunding for one. Investors invest in projects while people invest in people. The spirit of your pitch, perks, and promotion should be all you, and if you give to those potential contributors a piece of you, they'll give you more than just a piece of their paycheck. They'll give you the power you need to *really* succeed.

Chapter Sixteen

● ● ●

"I'm Not Only the Director, I'm Also a Contributor!"

SOME OF YOU might remember the 1980s TV commercial for the Hair Club for Men, where spokesperson Cy Sperling utters one of the most iconic concluding statements in TV history: "I'm not only the Hair Club president, but I'm also a client." Aside from this commercial being completely dated, it does bring up an interesting question for crowdfunders to consider: Should you contribute to your own film campaign? There is no right answer to this question. I've seen plenty of campaigns come and go, successful and unsuccessful. Some of the campaigners had indeed contributed money to their own campaign and others had not invested anything except time.

So if it doesn't make a difference to the success or failure of a crowdfunding campaign, then why am I even mentioning this? These chapters have all been about personalization and the integrity of a film campaign. Personalization means more than simply giving a piece of yourself to your film campaign; sometimes it means giving a part of what's yours — your time, energy, passion, and oftentimes sleeping hours — to your campaign. It may also mean putting your own hard-earned money where your mouth is. You're going to other people for the money you need to finance your film, so you should be willing to do the same, to set an example before anyone else does. That shows integrity.

Surprisingly, this is something crowdfunders rarely do. Let's be honest — if you are not willing to put *your* money into *your* own campaign, how can you ask any of your friends and family members to contribute, let alone a perfect stranger? Whether it's $5 or $5,000, you should be the one to kick-start your own campaign either by setting aside your own cash and raising additional funds, or by contributing immediately to your own campaign. I might suggest avoiding the latter choice only because then your $500 will be added to the total, which gets a percentage taken out of it by your crowdfunding platform, not to mention bank and other fees that will bring down your total amount disbursed. Therefore, you should keep your own monetary investment as untainted as possible.

With *Cerise*, I opted for the first choice and saved $10,000 of my own money, then crowdfunded an additional $5,000 more. I let my potential funders know this fact within the first thirty seconds of my pitch video, naturally. If you prefer the second choice, your name should definitely appear in your "Funders" or "Backers" tab, as opposed to being listed as "Anonymous," so that others know you're not only the campaigner, but you're also a contributor. This kind of *transparency* is vital to the integrity and ultimate success of your campaign.

Another important factor to consider in terms of integrity is that if you're not willing to spend money on your own film project and instead spend your money on other, more personal things, it can give potential contributors a negative impression of you and hinder some of them from becoming more than potential. This can be especially hazardous in a society that has gotten used to Tweeting whatever's on its mind.

For instance, while an acquaintance of mine who's married, has a child, and a house was crowdfunding for his film project, he was Tweeting about how he was going to take his family on a vacation. Granted, he works hard and deserves a vacation, like anyone else, but not while you're in the middle of a crowdfunding campaign. So much for the element of passion that so many potential contributors are drawn to in a project. Couple that with the fact that he put himself under a bit of scrutiny — people most likely began to wonder just how much he really wanted to make this film if he was not willing to put any of his own money into it and would rather take a vacation instead. It's really no wonder why he didn't even reach the halfway point of his crowdfunding goal during his campaign. I, for one, wasn't going to fund his film.

The *Te* of your campaign can suffer greatly due to this kind of twitless behavior, and if your integrity suffers, more than likely your credibility may begin to falter as well. You'll wind up with a lot more potential contributors not realizing their full promise with respect to your project. Before you know it, you'll be scrambling to raise the bulk of your funds in the final days and hours of your campaign.

Of course, not everyone raising money on Indiegogo or Kickstarter is concerned about integrity. They'll still launch a campaign and walk away with the funds necessary to put together a quality film project and not spend any time nurturing the relationships that helped get them to that point. Keep in mind, however, that crowdfunding may not be a one-time enterprise for you. If it works for one project, it may work again for another, and more than likely you'll be going back to the same core of contributors, supporters, friends, and family members for help. Therefore, it's important to keep yourself looking as much like a real mensch as possible throughout your campaign, especially on the social networks, with every email you send, and in your pitch video and any other video updates you do. Show yourself to be a good person who deserves a chance to realize his or her dreams as a filmmaker and you'll bring in more than money every time.

Chapter Seventeen

. . .

"BE WATER, MY FRIEND..." – TRANSPARENCY IS CLEAR AND COOL

IMMORTAL MARTIAL ARTIST, actor, and philosopher Bruce Lee spent much time perfecting himself in the physical world, as evidenced by some of his greatest films like *Enter the Dragon* and *Fist of Fury*, but also within the spiritual realm by studying various philosophies like Taoism and Buddhism. It's clear that Lee understood the importance of flow in the physical and ethereal planes, and it was with this in mind that he spoke what has become one of his most meaningful quotations:

> Be formless... shapeless, like water. Now you put water into a cup, it becomes the cup. You pour water into a bottle; it becomes the bottle. You put water into a teapot; it becomes the teapot. Now water can flow, or creep or drip or crash! Be water, my friend...

In the crowdfunding plane, you are the water, so pour yourself into it fully, and in the same way you would pour yourself into a film or screenplay. As I mentioned before, filmmakers often rush into crowdfunding with the sole idea that it is a hassle. They'd rather be working on their films, sketching out storyboards, or creating shot lists. All of this will happen in due time, but if your mind is on something other than the task at hand, that task will undoubtedly be compromised. Sometimes we take the shape of a director, other times a cinematographer, perhaps, but whatever we do, in order to do it right, we must allow ourselves to fill in every crevice of that title or job description and give that particular job 100% of ourselves for the time being.

Flow is a much more important aspect of crowdfunding than most people realize. Soon after you set up your campaign, personalize your pitch and perks, launch your campaign, and start promoting it, you'll notice whether all is going well. That's flow. If your campaign is faltering a short time into it, you should probably question why. Most of the time it's because you, the crowdfunder, are not putting all of yourself into campaigning. Perhaps you're working a day job, which is a reasonable necessity. You may have family to take care of, which, again, is another understandable necessity. You may enjoy sleep, which is again understandable. But the fact is that if you're pouring yourself into a few different glasses all at once, none of those glasses can ever hope to become filled with the potential they deserve because you only have so much water to give.

Going with the flow means necessity, and crowdfunding should become, at least for the months you're doing it, just as important a necessity as work and family and sleep. Crowdfunding for your film must become the glass that gets filled closest to the top. Like Bruce Lee says, "Water can flow or it can crash," and a surefire way to make it crash is to try and do too much with the limited time you have to crowdfund your film project.

Water not only flows and takes the shape of the thing it's poured into, but it's also transparent, and transparency is perhaps the most essential element of crowdfunding. Since crowdfunding is online fundraising, most of the money you receive from contributors will be made online via PayPal or Amazon. What happens if you bring a little money in from a friend who isn't especially techno-savvy and doesn't want to contribute to your campaign through an online payment platform, so instead hands you $100 in cash or as a check? How do you report that to Kickstarter or Indiegogo? More importantly, how do you report that to your online contributors?

When I crowdfunded for *Cerise*, I raised a very small amount of money from external sources, namely a couple of former students of mine, one who contributed $10 and another who contributed a slightly more substantial amount. The first thing I learned is that you should be honest about receiving funds in this way. Granted, there's really no way for your contributors to find out that you brought in additional money behind the scenes unless you tell them, but in this way, your integrity as a crowdfunder stays intact and you show yourself to be sincere and trustworthy with other people's money.

Nowadays, you can actually add any additional amounts of money you raise separately from your online campaigning on most crowdfunding platforms, so it's much easier to keep your campaign like water. The minute we do something as crowdfunders that puts us under the scrutiny of our supporters and contributors, it's very difficult to rebound. Again, it's about keeping your *Te* intact for this and future crowdfunding endeavors, and that means bending when the road before you bends instead of trying too hard to continue straight ahead. In short, you should always go with the natural flow of crowdfunding to avoid any possible pitfalls and plummets along the way.

Chapter Eighteen

• • •

A PRACTICAL GUIDE TO CROWDFUNDER ETIQUETTE

SOME OF YOU might be thinking, *I didn't know such a thing as crowdfunder etiquette existed!* Well, it does or it doesn't, depending on your own experiences with crowdfunding and/or contributing to a campaign or two. I prefer to call it by its more common name: *good manners.* Whether your crowdfunding platform is Indiegogo, Kickstarter, or any of the others on the Internet, here are a few basic tenets every campaigner should strive to always uphold.

SAYING PLEASE AND THANK YOU

A good friend of mine who had successfully crowdfunded for his feature-length film brought this to my attention as one of his pet peeves. He mentioned that he had contributed to a few film projects, and the campaigners didn't even Tweet a simple "thank you" for his pledges. I couldn't believe it. I thought to myself, *Would someone really not thank a complete stranger for giving money to his or her project?* Apparently, it happens, and it's audacious and will most surely end one's future as a crowdfunder.

As a crowdfunder, you should thank each and every contributor to your film campaign. It's really the absolute least you can do to show your appreciation for them coming to bat for your project and for you. Sending an email, a message on Facebook, and/or a direct message on Twitter is fine, too, though in today's multifaceted social network, the more out in the open your "thank you" is, the better.

A great example of a very simple thank-you status update is this one from Kris and Lindy Boustedt for their film campaign for *This Is Ours.* On Facebook, they thanked a contributor by stating, "Backer

134 is the talented local actress Darlene Sellers. Thank you Darlene!" While this is a fine thank you, you can, of course, get even more personal and at times pretty creative with your thank-you Tweets and updates. For instance, the guys and girls behind the zombie film spoof *Red Scare* kept true to their campaign strategy in their thank you, maintaining the 1950s-style "Patriotic America" motif and, of course, silly humor: "We all knew she was a real American hero... but now we know she's even Americaner. Hilda Rozas. Thank you."

Also, think of the benefit of thanking someone up close and personally. If you thank contributors more directly for all your social networks to see, that will most likely pave the way to further contributions, especially if you're thanking a fair amount of people per day. Plus, this behavior of exercising good manners will also help build up what Slava Rubin at Indiegogo calls your "social proof," which we'll touch more on later. But beware: If other contributors unearth the dark truth that a humble contributor gave even as little as $5 to your project and you *didn't* thank them, watch out!

THANK YOUR OTHER SUPPORTERS

Not everyone is going to have even $5 to contribute to your crowdfunding campaign, no matter how awesome your project is going to be, or no matter how much they would like to give money to it. People who can't contribute financially to a campaign tend to support you in other ways, mainly by getting the word out about your project to their friends and followers, some of whom may be able to fork up the money, get a cool perk, and have the honor of saying they're a contributor to this project.

So apart from thanking actual contributors, it's equally as important to thank any- and everybody who supports your project in other ways. Those who retweet your Tweets about your film campaign or share your Kickstarter link on Google Plus and Facebook deserve a little recognition from the campaign owner. It's polite and shows them that you appreciate their part in getting the word out about your film project. If you thank them the first time and subsequently, they will be more likely to keep up awareness about your project in their social universe.

Again, here's another prime example of a heartfelt Twitter thank you from @samplat (Sam Platizky of *Red Scare*):

Trigonis John T. Trigonis
Commie zombies want your brains! So help the boys @Blame_Romero capture 'em (on film!) Support #RedScare today: http://bit.ly /ScaredRed
13 Jun

in reply to ↑

@Samplat
Sam Platizky

thanks, @Trigonis for your support !! @Blame_Romero

13 Jun via web

☆ Favorite ⎏ Retweet ↰ Reply

Red Scare's Sam Platizky (@samplat) *shows his appreciation for my promoting his zombie feature in a kind thank-you Tweet.*

Another example is a Tweet from Leilani Holmes (@momentsof-film), which reads, "Thanks to everyone who's been RT-ing our Indiegogo campaign for #ClowningAroundFilm. You Rock Our Big Red Noses!" Heartfelt and relevant to the campaign for Damien Cullen's short film *Clowning Around* about two clowns battling to be *the* Bozo of the Big Top.

THE "MAGIC WORD" STILL WORKS MAGIC

While urgency is understandable, especially when crowdfunding in an "All or Nothing" fashion, your Tweets and updates, email blasts, and other forms of online promotion should still employ the word "please" whenever possible, or its popular abbreviations "pls" or "plz." No one wants to feel as though you are demanding a contribution and support. The word "please" softens this determination ever so slightly while demonstrating a certain element of humility in a campaigner, which can go a very long way with crowdfunding.

SEND YOUR CONTRIBUTORS SOMETHING NOW AND LATER

Ralph Waldo Emerson once wrote, "With the past, I have nothing to do; nor with the future. I live now," and so do the people who contribute to your film campaign. Therefore, you should give them something more immediate than a signed copy of the DVD when the film's finished several months after your campaign has ended. As

My Sync perks — a pair of records and a nifty sticker!

I already mentioned, whenever possible this perk should be personalized for the contributor at one of your lower perk levels, and somehow related to your film project, like the awesome perks from *Sync* seen at the bottom of page 90.

I contributed to Brendon's short film, and then received my perks — a pair of records from Brendon's personal collection (he threw in the Idris Muhammad record because he couldn't decide which to send between that and Sammy Davis Jr.) and a pair of *Sync* stickers — a couple of weeks after I clicked "Contribute Now" on the project's Indiegogo page. I now had a constant reminder of *Sync* until the film was finished and I received my DVD copy in the mail at a later date.

A sound designer named Christopher Postill reached out to me about his Indiegogo project *Sounds Like an Earful*, a podcast about getting people to rethink the sounds they're surrounded by on a daily basis. I examined his campaign, and, seeing the usual suspects of perks, I suggested he personalize them for his potential funders. I also suggested he offer something more immediate to keep his contributors listening until the first episode of the podcast was launched. When I looked at his campaign's homepage a few days later, I noticed he'd added a perk in which he would create a sound specifically for the funder. Another perk higher up the ladder features Christopher creating a piece of music that the funder can gift to a friend or family member.

Not only are these two new perks innovative and personal, offering contributors a piece of Christopher's world of sound, but they're also *immediate*. Once they're created, they can be posted to the funder's Facebook wall, Tweeted, and/or emailed. Again, from there, friends of those funders can listen to the music and say to themselves, "Man, I want a piece of music made just for me!" Then they can visit *Sounds Like an Earful*'s Indiegogo page and click "Contribute Now."

These are the basics of crowdfunder etiquette, which is really about making people feel appreciated by publicly acknowledging them for all the good things they're doing on your behalf. Nothing builds up more *Te* than being a grateful, humble person. And building up integrity is what it takes to not only get through one crowdfunding campaign, but to build a reputation as a fine paradigm of what a crowdfunder *should* be, a person who understands how to treat his or her contributors and supporters, as well as the community as a whole.

· PART THREE ·
SUMMARY POINTS

- A successful film campaign begins with the three Ps of crowdfunding — pitch, perks, and promotion — and is enhanced by the fourth P: personalization.

- Your pitch should include an introduction, the pitch itself, and the showcase. The pitch can be further broken down to include a précis, purpose, and perks.

- Investors give to projects, people give to people.

- Transparency is a key element in any crowdfunding campaign, so be sure contributors and supporters see all of your behind-the-scenes activities.

- Crowdfunder etiquette, or good manners, includes basics like saying please and thank you and sending your contributors something for the present and the future.

• Part Three •
EXERCISES

1. Draft a pitch which includes an introduction (who you are), the pitch, which explains what your film is about (précis), why you're crowdfunding (purpose), and what some of your perks are (perks), and a list of prior work through which you'd like to showcase your talent.

2. Start now: Set aside a small amount of money from your biweekly paycheck from now until you're ready to launch your crowdfunding campaign. This way, you can proclaim in your pitch video, "I'm not only the director, I'm also a contributor."

3. Take a moment to think about some of your perks. Which ones can you gear toward your potential contributors? What can you offer immediately? Are your perks relevant to your film project?

PART COMMUNITY
4 ENGAGEMENT

Chapter Nineteen

. . .

PU: LET YOUR COMMUNITY HELP CARVE YOUR UNCARVED BLOCK

EVERYONE'S PROBABLY HEARD THE PHRASE "no one's an island" before, and this is very true with crowdfunding. The same way you should avoid jumping into a film campaign without a proper team or a set strategy, you should avoid thinking you can do this alone. The very nature of crowdfunding dictates that you can't. Without an actual crowd coming together for the common purpose of your project, no money could be raised and your film would remain on the page, perhaps indefinitely.

Your crowdfunding campaign can be compared to an uncarved block — or *Pu* — that needs to be carved into something. According to Lao Tzu in the *Tao Te Ching*, we are the essence of *Pu* when we are born, and through time and experience, we allow the world to carve us into who and what we are meant to be. The difficulty lies in staying receptive to the natural flow of the world around us. With crowdfunding, your film campaign is the uncarved block, and though we think we as campaigners have full control over the fate of our campaigns and film projects, that's only partially true. A successful campaign depends not only on its campaigner, but on the community as well.

Indiegogo has an acronym to describe this: *DIWO*, or *Do It With Others*. This is the core of crowdfunding — community engagement. Just as you might set up a lemonade stand as a child and expect your closest neighbors and members of your immediate family to be among the first to walk on over and buy one for a buck, you can expect the same from your immediate online community. This is especially true today. If you have an original product, a local homemade brew of beer, for instance, you will attract the attention of your surrounding community. Because this brew is "local" and "homemade," people will be more likely to give their money to your brand as opposed to picking up another domestic beer like Yuengling that's brewed in the next state over. If your product is well received, that same community will start talking and spread the word about this awesome, local beer to others.

This is a very organic means by which to get your project to stretch out across the country, even the world, in an online sense. Just like the local brewer probably doesn't have the finances to physically market his or her beer to bars and lounges all over the US, most DIY filmmakers don't have the means to spread the word about their projects through business cards, printed full-color posters, and other promotional materials, and instead rely on a fully digital form of grassroots word-of-mouth campaigning through their online community. But first you have to build that community and make them care about your particular project.

If you have a solid film project on your hands and are passionate about getting that product into the world, the people in your community will come to your aid, sometimes with not only money, but perhaps with their time and other services that may ultimately help you with your campaign and your finished film. Though we may feel that DIY filmmaking is really doing it ourselves, it doesn't have to be. Here's how to make your community care about you, your campaign, and, above all, your film project.

Chapter Twenty

• • •

THE GOLDEN RULE: "DON'T SOLICIT, ELICIT"

COMMUNITY IS A POWERFUL TOOL when it comes to helping spread the word about your crowdfunding campaign on your social networks. Perhaps the greatest aspect of community is that in most cases it *will* come to bat for you when you need it most. It can be that friend who lends you his or her couch for a month while you're looking for a new apartment, or that trusted professor who'll take time out of his or her day and write up a recommendation letter you need to send to some graduate school the following morning.

As with anything or anyone, you have to know how to make them want to help you. More often than not, you may be able to go to a family member or a good friend and ask them for something directly. But what about random people, some of whom may be strangers or at best friends of friends twice removed by way of the Internet? How do you ask them for a contribution to your film campaign and at the same time make them actually want to contribute?

I find my Twitter feed frequently bombarded by crowdfunding campaigns all vying for attention amidst hundreds of followers. For those of us in the indie film community, this has become a common occurrence. During the first years of the crowdfunding boom, what I found cluttering my feed were repetitious "Help make it happen for" Tweets and those punctuated by a "please RT," which asks anyone who reads this Tweet to retweet (RT) it to their followers in an attempt to further the campaigner's outreach. I'm happy to report that the latter of those two trends has fallen out of vogue; and while there's nothing wrong with Tweets of this sort, the drawbacks are that they don't (1) make me want to retweet them; (2) make me want to check out the campaign; or (3) make me care anything about the project. I might look at it simply because I know the person behind the campaign or retweet, but that may not be a good enough reason for most people to help spread the word or contribute.

When you *elicit* help, on the other hand, it makes the community want to support you and spread the word about your project. The prime difference between soliciting and eliciting is that when you solicit something, you simply ask for it head on, whereas when you elicit something, you're evoking a reaction from another person. It means the difference between this Tweet by James Huffman soliciting help for his film *Trails of Gray* about a careworn couple who goes hiking to find closure — "Good morning! Make a donation today for @Trailsofgray. Help make it happen at @Indiegogo" — and this one from Shane Monahan and his film *Musket* eliciting support from the crowd — "Sure, we could've put the script on the shelf, but we believe in #Musket and #indiefilm! Every buck helps!" A little personality will always go the distance.

Here's this difference illustrated in a more practical setting: You see your friend thoroughly enjoying a piece of steak, cooked just the way you like it. It's dripping with juices and smells unbearably delicious. So you *ask* him, "Can I have a piece of your steak?" to which your friend now has the option to say yay or nay. Your friend has the power over you. Now, if you look at that steak and salivate over it — well, that won't work either because that's just sad. But if you look up from that magnificent bit of medium-well goodness and say to your friend something along the lines of, "Man, that steak looks and smells delicious!" as a statement, you will *elicit* a reaction from your friend, which will most likely be "It is…" (wait for it) "… Do you want to try a piece?" Now you've got the power and soon after, a tasty piece of steak.

With regard to crowdfunding and bringing in contributions as well as your community's help, you want to evoke in them the feeling that they *need* to help you and your campaign in some way. That's where you can get a little creative with your Tweets, since eliciting a reaction from people is not an easy task, and to evoke a response that's strong enough to get them to give you money can be even trickier. This is why many crowdfunders I know succumb to the solicitation method — it's much easier to simply ask and in the next minute either see a retweet or not, or see a spike in your total funds raised. Or not. (More on this in Chapter Twenty-Seven.)

An acquaintance of mine ran an unsuccessful campaign for his feature-length film, and three days before the conclusion of his campaign, he submitted an article he wrote to Film Courage outlining the five things he learned from crowdfunding. One of his "sobering realities" was that "just because you support them, don't assume they will support you," and of course this is true. In terms of contributing money to a campaign, there are a ton of variables to consider. In terms of other types of support, however, you as the crowdfunder should show people a good enough reason for them to care about your project. If you do, they will feel compelled to support you. Admittedly, this happens to me with very few projects, but when a campaigner compels me to support his or her film project, I don't just append an "RT" to the original Tweet. I craft my own Tweet as a testament to just how much this person had moved me to pitch in.

As I've mentioned a few times before, Lucas McNelly's *A Year Without Rent* had been stagnant for the long haul of the campaign but found success in its final days and hours. This video project was pulled out of the Sarlacc pit of unfunded dreams by the strength of the entire indie film community. This is an exceptional case, as I *do not* recommend starting a campaign without plenty of preparation and a solid plan of action plotted out beforehand, but the lesson is standard: *If you show passion for your project and a willingness to drive it forward even in the face of failure, your community will more than likely come to your aid.*

About a year after my crowdfunding campaign for *Cerise* ended and the film was primed and ready for festival submissions, I decided to launch a series of "Crusades for *Cerise*," in which I'd seek film festival submission funds from friends and followers. Whenever I would promote a given Crusade, I made sure each Tweet and status update on Facebook was unique and cleverly worded. Sure enough, my followers retweeted it to their followers. I never had to ask anyone to "please RT" because I had also built up some credibility by showing them that I take pride not only in my film but also in every minute detail that makes up the whole of *Cerise*, from crowdfunding campaign to production and ultimately to my Crusades.

Another way to elicit a boost to the awareness factor of your project on social networks and even further out is to try and land some interviews and spots on the various Internet radio shows. Plenty of filmmakers and film enthusiasts run weekly shows on Blog Talk Radio like Miles Maker's *Convercinema*, Rex Sikes' *Movie Beat*, and Talkshoe's *Cutting Room Floor* with Casey Ryan. There's also the inimitable *FilmSnobbery* and the prestigious *Film Courage*, which airs on LA Talk Radio. If you're doing a good job with your campaigning and standing out amidst the flood of crowdfunding campaigns rushing down your Twitter and Facebook feeds, you'll nab the attention of these influencers, like I did, which can spread out your crowdfunding campaign to an even wider audience, and maybe even attract the attention of some major players as well.

The more you practice the art of elicitation, the easier it will become to bring together a community invested in the welfare of your film campaign, and the more instrumental they will be in helping you carve out a successful campaign and leading you toward a crowdfunding victory. With all the crowdfunding traffic circulating in the vastness of the Internet, and especially all over the social networks, you must stand out not only with your film premise and campaign strategy, but also with each and every aspect of your promotion.

People forget things; if they see you're reaching out for a retweet and you give them the chance to think to themselves, *I'll retweet this later,* chances are they won't. Your Tweets should therefore be compelling enough to make the person stop whatever he or she is doing and lend a helping hand to you and your campaign immediately.

Chapter Twenty-One

• • •

THE IMPORTANCE OF KEEPING YOUR CONTRIBUTORS UPDATED

MATTHEW BRODERICK SAID IT BEST in *Ferris Bueller's Day Off*: "Life moves pretty fast. If you don't stop and look around once in a while, you could miss it." That was back in 1986. Today, the world moves inconceivably fast, and this is especially true for the entertainment industry, indie or otherwise. The advent of social networking has even made information flow at real-time speeds. Many of us do our best to keep up with this rushing tide and at the same time try to create our own fresh content so we have something meaningful to share with the world.

Keeping people updated about your film project is integral to the lifespan of your crowdfunding campaign. This is especially true with regard to your contributors, since they have some stake in seeing how the film turns out. Whether they're actual investors, as per the JOBS Act, or everyday Joes and Janes donating money for particular perks, most contributors don't give money and then forget about your project. They want to see what is released into the world once the film is complete, so keep them updated about every aspect of your project, from crowdfunding to film festival screenings.

There are many ways to do this, and with so many variables, we can quickly become overwhelmed. Questions will pile up: How many email blasts are too many? What's the right number of social networking sites to keep active on? When should I set up my film's website? These are just a few of the topics that, when fixated on, can hinder a successful campaign, so I've included some principal methods of keeping your contributors, followers, and friends updated with the goings-on of your crowdfunding campaign.

EMAIL BLASTS: TRIED AND TESTED

At one point during my crowdfunding seminar at Golden Door International Film Festival of Jersey City, my cohost, Indiegogo's own Slava Rubin, posed a question to the audience: Which method brings in the most money: email, Facebook, or Twitter? The majority of the audience (myself included) said Twitter. Some others raised their hands in praise of Facebook. Practically no one chose the correct answer, which is email. We've gotten so hung up on social networking that we sometimes forget that email is really the progenitor of all modern modes of communication.

You should send your contributors updates via email at least once a month. With *Cerise*, I sent out occasional email blasts to my modest network, keeping them in the know about how close I was getting to my $5,000 target. Many of them would see that yesterday the number was at $2,350 and today it had jumped to $2,700. When your network sees that people are supporting your project financially, they may be more likely to put in $5 or $10 since "everyone else is doing it."

This goes back to the idea of building up your social proof. According to data from Indiegogo, if a campaign reaches 30 or 40% of its crowdfunding goal, strangers will start contributing to the project. By strangers, I don't mean your close friends on your contact list, since they should be among the first to contribute. I mean those who are more professional contacts, the ones you don't lunch with on a weekly basis. Show them that others are doing it, and they will do it, too.

SOCIAL NETWORKING

As easy as it may be to update your Facebook status and send out a Tweet, people who are new to social networking will realize that there are a ton of sites out there, some for general and professional contacts like LinkedIn, and others specified for the film and entertainment industry. In fact, most websites nowadays have a social media component; even Kickstarter has jumped on the bandwagon, allowing you to follow certain contributors and see what projects they're currently backing. These websites require visitors to sign in, create a profile, upload a profile pic, and start sharing. Facebook Connect makes it even easier and quicker to get started using one of these websites.

The ultimate question is this: How can I possibly keep my contributors updated on all of these social networking websites? The answer is simple: you can't. I attended a panel discussion about social media and filmmaking, and one of the panelists, Leslie Poston, author of *Social Media Metrics for Dummies*, coauthor of *Twitter for Dummies,* and the head of Magnitude Media, a company that specializes in social media and business branding, said that a person should be active on no more than five social media sites in order to maximize one's content output. Coming from someone who is well over 60,000 Tweets strong, I'd put my money on that answer.

Once you've chosen your five social networks, you can then friend your contributors and keep them updated a bit more than once a month. I told contributors in an early email that if they want monthly updates, they should visit *Cerise's* website or subscribe to its RSS feed for regular updates; if they want more frequent updates, they should add me as a friend on Facebook; if they want real time updates, Twitter's the way to go. By wording it this way, you give your contributors the choice of how they'd like to be updated about your project, which makes it about them.

You might also want to consider creating a separate Twitter handle for your film like @TilttheMovie and @Blame_Romero did, if separation of filmmaker from film is something that's important to you. But again, by doing this, you add more to your plate when the very essence of *Pu* is simplicity. Therefore, keep it simple. I didn't have the need to create @CeriseMovie for Twitter because for a time that was the only interesting thing I was Tweeting about, so *Cerise* quickly became synonymous with my personal Twitter handle. And since personalization is what this kind of campaigning is about, it was a fine fit for *Cerise* and others like it and may be for your film campaign as well.

FILM WEBSITES, BLOGS, AND OTHER WAYS TO UPDATE

Now you're ready to move into the big time. Eventually, your film, whether still in the crowdfunding stages or packaged and ready for film festival submissions, will need a website that offers basic information: a synopsis, director's statement, cast and crew list, some production stills, and a trailer. On most websites, there's a "News" section as well, which is good for updates about all that's happening with your film for people discovering your movie for the first time.

Years ago, setting up a website was an incredibly expensive endeavor. Add to that the cost of a webmaster to maintain your site and keep it updated. Today, there are new DIY ways to keep costs low so you don't need a separate crowdfunding campaign for website funds. One of the latest trends is customizing a blog site like WordPress or Tumblr. By taking this route, you get a functional website with free hosting. In fact, all you'd really have to pay for is a domain name, since not many filmmakers would want a URL to read http://cerisemovie.wordpress.com. The best part is that if you customize the website enough, there's really no telling a blog-based web page from a more "legit" one. The website for *Cerise* is not much more than a modified WordPress page:

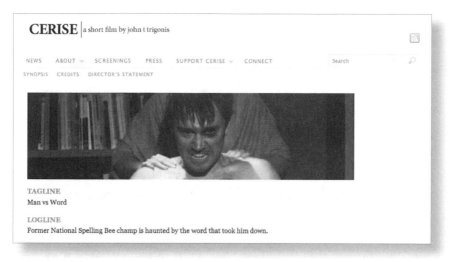

For Cerise's website, I used a customized WordPress. For a short film, a blog site works perfectly fine.

Splashy Flash pages with animated graphics should be reserved for Hollywood movies. A website for an indie short or feature-length film should be informational at the very least, which means a blog page will work wonders. For added pizazz, many of these blog sites allow you to upload your own background photos and designs to further appeal to people visiting your page for the first time. For further options for customization, however, you may be required to move from the free tier to the paid tier. All in all, it will still be much less expensive than setting up an actual website.

NOW THAT IT'S OVER...

Even after you've crowdfunded like a rock star for three intense months, thanked all your contributors, and mailed away their perks, you're only just beginning to see the finish line. The same way it's important to keep your contributors updated throughout your campaign, it's just as important to maintain a steady flow of updates about the progress of your film project after the campaign has ended. Your contributors have funded your campaign for various reasons, so the least you should do is make them feel like they're a part of something bigger than themselves because to many of them, helping to fund a film is a big deal.

Perhaps *Cerise* funder Andrew Bichler says it best in a short video about why he contributed to my short film: "What really turned me on [was] the fact that I, as an everyday guy, could get involved in funding and supporting the arts…" You heard it right from a proud funder's mouth. As such, it's gratifying to be kept in the loop about what's going on regarding a project you've become an integral part of. I receive regular updates with behind-the-scenes footage, post-production notes, and other status updates from many of the projects I've contributed to like *Red Scare*, *Tilt*, and *How Do You Write a Joe Schermann Song*. If you don't update your audience, they may start to think all kinds of outrageous things, the worst of which quite possibly being, *Well, I won't support that person's campaigns anymore!*

Again, it's all about appreciation, so you should treat your contributors with the same high level of respect you might show an investor whether he or she has contributed at the $1 rung or higher up toward the top of the crowdfunding ladder.

Chapter Twenty-Two

• • •

AVOID "THE FLOOD"

WHEN COMPANIES ATTEMPT to engage their customers too frequently or forcefully, it ultimately leads to disengagement. Taoism is all about balance. When crowdfunding for and promoting your film project, you need to maintain a solid line between getting the word out about your campaign to potential contributors and being a pest. With crowdfunding, it should also be mentioned that you are approaching people who haven't signed up for it. Therefore, if you cross that line, your contacts may be less likely to trust you than they might a tried and tested clothing company like Old Navy.

Even though every drop in a body of water is unique, when viewed collectively in large volume, that singularity disappears and we're left with just water. The same holds true for the following two ways that are certain to flood away your supporters.

EMAIL INUNDATION

As mentioned in the previous chapter, email blasts can be a great tool for both promoting your crowdfunding campaign and keeping your contributors and email contacts updated. As with anything, though, too much is too much, and you should find a balance and strive to keep it. This doesn't necessarily mean you should only send out a blast zealously on the second Tuesday of every month. That's not balance, either, because what if something extraordinary happens in the interim? In today's e-world, "yesterday's news is tomorrow's fish and chip paper," to borrow a line from an Elvis Costello song. When something happens this morning, it's old news by the afternoon.

Email blasts should therefore be sent out strategically and never, never once a day, since even that can be construed by most as a nuisance, and you will get the inevitable email that crowdfunders dread: "Please unsubscribe me from this email, thank you." And, of course, not every email will be this kindly worded.

SOCIAL DELUGE

Flooding your social feed with the same material can oftentimes lead to unfollowing on Twitter, unfriending on Facebook, and unpleasantries in general. I see this at times from crowdfunders, as well as some of the more hardcore supporters of crowdfunding, many of whom can't contribute to a given film campaign so they overcompensate by boosting their level of social support to the status of "annoying."

On page 113 is an example of this type of constant Tweeting from A. D. Lane, who's been crowdfunding for his feature-length film *Invasion of the Not Quite Dead* since May of 2009, campaigning 24/7 (almost literally!) and independent of any crowdfunding intermediaries.

While this isn't such a terrible thing for crowdfunders themselves, and especially Lane, who's raised almost £100,000 as of May 2012 solely on Twitter, it can be quite a hassle to scroll through if you have friends who only go on Facebook to see what their friends are doing. It may be annoying for them to speed past an abundance of updates and Indiegogo or Kickstarter links. It can be (and has been) grounds for unfriending and unfollowing, truth be told. Therefore, you should keep aware of how many times per day you promote your campaign and, of course, keep a balance between your personal and your crowdfunding lives.

> **AD Lane (Filmmaker)** @indywoodFILMS   2h
> our WEEKEND FILM FUNDRAISER is currently at £20, please help us
> get this to £100 this next hour, U can DONATE/UPGRADE @
> indywood.co.uk

> **AD Lane (Filmmaker)** @indywoodFILMS   2h
> in the meantime, please keep backing our film project at
> indywood.co.uk & help us have a successful fundraising day... thanks
> guys...

> **AD Lane (Filmmaker)** @indywoodFILMS   2h
> YAY... I'm BACK home at INDYWOOD HQ... just unpacking... so I'll be
> around a lot more later...

> **AD Lane (Filmmaker)** @indywoodFILMS   3h
> We are making a horror film that is 100% twitter fan funded... pls help
> us out @ indywood.co.uk...

> **AD Lane (Filmmaker)** @indywoodFILMS   3h
> Who is going to be amazing and add to our Fridays total of £20
> raised? Check out movie perks @ indywood.co.uk...

> **AD Lane (Filmmaker)** @indywoodFILMS   4h
> Pls support my independent horror film, 100% funded by YOU...
> check it out @ indywood.co.uk...

> **Carly Street** @carlystreet2010   4h
> Special #FF @indywoodFILMS breaking down the barriers of the
> industry! Stop by indywood.co.uk and find out how you can help! :D
> ↻ Retweeted by AD Lane (Filmmaker)
> ↩ In reply to AD Lane (Filmmaker)

A. D. Lane's nonstop Tweeting for his feature-length film Invasion of the Not Quite Dead.

DAM IT!

But let's be realistic: Crowdfunding means marketing. So how can we find this much-needed balance? With regard to email blasts, you can set up a separate account for your film via your website or create a separate email account and import your contacts. The one thing you'll have to be sure to do, of course, is to mention this in your first email blast from that account so that people don't automatically put a block on an email from an unknown source. Also, people can opt out early on in case they're not interested in your crowdfunding campaign but still would like to keep you as their contact.

A simple fix for your social flooding problems is to designate different social networking sites for different purposes. For instance, you may notice that Facebook and Google Plus share the same features with only a few exceptions. Why post your campaign's link on both Facebook and Google Plus when chances are your Facebook friends and Google Plus circles are comprised of the same network of people? Because Google Plus has a more professional appearance than Facebook, you might choose to use it exclusively for posting updates about your project, your pitch video, and all other aspects of your crowdfunding campaign, leaving Facebook for updates about any other goings-on in your life, with perhaps an occasional mention of your campaign mixed in here and there.

Of all the social networking sites, Twitter is probably the best hybrid for both business and personal interaction with your following, so you shouldn't run into any issues posting personal thoughts and opinions as well as promotional information about your crowdfunding campaign. You may choose to only promote your film's campaign on Twitter, which appears to be a solid idea, looking at A. D. Lane's campaign as a prime example. As of May 2012, he had a massive following of over 101,000 people watching and waiting to see how "the world's first 100% Twitter fan-funded horror film trilogy" turns out when it's all over.

Charlie Chaplin says it best in his famous speech at the end of *The Great Dictator*: "You are not machines... you are men!" (And women!) That said, you should not flood your feed with Tweets and updates exclusively about your campaign, no matter how creatively worded they may be. The objects of marketing in crowdfunding are to raise funds, build a community comprised of contributors and supporters to help make your campaign stronger, and intricately carve out of that *Pu* a masterpiece of a campaign — and not disfigure it with quantity lacking quality.

Chapter Twenty-Three

• • •

"I'VE GOT NO MONEY, BUT I CAN GIVE _____!"

HERE'S A FACT that crowdfunders don't like to admit: sometimes people really don't have any money to give to a film campaign. But there's more to crowdfunding than simply raising money and awareness. There's also the *crowdsourcing* element that sometimes gets lost in the world of crowdfunding. In a nutshell, crowdsourcing means reaching out to the crowd to obtain anything at all, not only the money you need to make your film. Crowdfunding can be about obtaining other things just as valuable, if not more so, than funding and free promotion.

For instance, because of his success crowdfunding *A Year Without Rent* on Kickstarter, Lucas McNelly attracted the attention of the entire indie film community, and thus became a collaborator on various other projects thanks to the very nature of *A Year Without Rent*. To be a filmmaker, you don't make just one film, you make *films*, so the more help you can attract, the more films you'll make. Lucas was able to attract influential film people like Ted Hope, as well as the attention of Internet websites like Film Threat and Mubi Garage. Aside from money and couches to sleep on, since the premise behind *A Year Without Rent* was for Lucas to tour around the country for a year helping filmmakers with their film projects, Lucas also landed a column on *Filmmaker Magazine*'s website where he could update everyone on all things related to his *Year Without Rent*.

Aside from collaborators on future film projects, filmmakers have also received press opportunities because of their crowdfunding campaigns. Sometimes, and especially if you're keeping a solid connection with prominent people on Facebook and Twitter, you can attract the attention of those Internet publications as well as Internet radio programs like *Cutting Room Floor* and *Rex Sikes' Movie Beat,* which I mentioned in the previous chapter. This kind of press can substantially boost awareness about your crowdfunding campaign and build up your credibility as well. A one-hour spot on *Film Courage* should be treated like a ten-minute spot on *The Late Show.*

Another prime example is film producer Sarah Marder, who received some really outstanding press in one of the country's most prestigious magazines — *The Atlantic* — for her documentary *The Genius of a Place*, which explores the intricate differences between an agrarian-based economy and one that can only thrive through tourism and commercialization. Aside from this notable feat of press, Sarah and her *Genius of a Place*, which surpassed its goal of $20,000 for finishing funds on Indiegogo, was also the subject of Episode 56 of the podcast *Eye on Italy*, since Sarah's documentary is centered in the small town of Cortona, Italy.

Whether it's big or small press, it's all press, and because of the Internet, any press has the ability to reach out further than it ever has before. The fact is you never know who's watching. Take Julie Keck and Jessica King, who penned the screenplay for the indie thriller and crowdfunding success story *Tilt*. The screenwriting duo known throughout the indie film community as King is a Fink are currently working on a plethora of projects: Jessica cowrote the narration for a documentary called *A Second Knock at the Door* with *Tilt* backer and director Chris Grimes while Julie handled the social media outreach, and now they are working together on another project for Chris's company 5414 Productions. They also wrote a live game show called *Who Knows Her Better* and a play/web series called *I Hate Tommy Finch*, both for Tello Films — they were introduced to Tello cofounder Christin Mell by another *Tilt* backer. Plus, the girls are working on two feature-length screenplays. All of this came about because people were paying attention to the *Tilt* campaign and saw the innovative things that Julie and Jessica were contributing to it, namely *Tilt* the Town.

Cerise was also on the receiving end of much kindness from one-time strangers who have now become close friends and supporters. Music has always been one of the more difficult things for me as a filmmaker to come by; it was especially difficult before the days of crowdfunding when all of my expenses were out-of-pocket and these pockets didn't run very deep. At one point during my campaign, I was messaging people on Facebook trying to elicit contributions. At the time, I didn't realize the silliness of messaging an indie rock band for a monetary handout — bands are basically pooling their money together to keep them rocking and rolling with their music. So when Kevin Adkins, lead singer/songwriter of Icewagon Flu, actually got in touch with me, I didn't know what to expect. He wrote that he and the band had no money to give, but he then asked if they could donate a song to *Cerise*. Immediately I responded with an emphatic "Yes! That would be awesome."

The band, whose song "Liza Was Rejected" appeared in my prior short film *Perfekt*, wrote up a song called "Cerise," which incorporates all the themes and ideas that I explore in the film. The music itself was quirky and fun, and I couldn't have been happier. And during the Big Apple preview of *Cerise*, Icewagon Flu made a guest appearance and played a short acoustic set of their songs, including "Cerise," right before we screened the film for an audience of 100 friends, family members, and Indiegogo funders.

Not only was I able to get an awesome, catchy title track for *Cerise*, but a few weeks after Icewagon Flu agreed to donate the song, a music composer from Serbia named Nino Rajacic reached out to me and asked if he could donate an entire score to the film. He had discovered my project on Indiegogo and said it sounded like a really cool concept — something he'd like to have in his credits. Without hesitation, we got to work a few weeks later sharing our ideas, and then Nino sat down and started composing the music. A few minor tweaks later, and *Cerise* had a wonderful score and Nino had some more cinematic music added to his resume. It was a win–win, and all because of crowdfunding.

Cerise also got its website from another funder named Ben Gerber, who initially contributed a substantial amount of money to the film's Indiegogo campaign. Then he asked Marinell and me if we were thinking of setting up a website, and when we told him we were, he brought his brother into the mix to work on designing one from a WordPress page. Once the website was up and running, Ben surprised us again a couple of weeks later with a domain name, and since then, he has also taken care of the web hosting fees so we can keep *cerisemovie.com* up and running all year round.

Money is the primary reason we filmmakers launch a crowdfunding campaign, but it's only part of the ongoing battle that is DIY film-making. There are so many other variables to take into consideration — from music to marketing, transmedia, and beyond — all of which would normally require time and money. However, you never know when someone like Nino may stumble on your project because of a Google search and contribute his editing or sound design skills pro bono simply because it seems like a worthwhile project. And if you create a strong enough buzz about your film campaign, you'll no doubt attract the attention of newspapers and magazines, the way Lucas and Sarah had done, or find future collaborators to work with and continue paving the road toward a successful career as a working filmmaker.

Chapter Twenty-Four

• • •

DON'T PANIC! — HANDLING "THE LULL" BETWEEN CONTRIBUTIONS

IT'S BOUND TO HAPPEN at least once in every crowdfunding campaign, no matter how expertly crafted and strategized it is. For a time you'll be on a roll, raking in contribution upon contribution. The communities you've reached out to will seem to be coming together in aid of your film project, sending out feelers amongst their own various networks and bringing in further funding to your campaign. Everything will be going smoothly. Maybe even just as planned.

And then, without warning, it will stop.

You may find yourself sitting in front of your computer at home or at the office refreshing your campaign's homepage only to verify an inconceivable truth: you're stuck at the same dollar amount, and you've been stuck at this same dollar amount for a few hours now. Perhaps even a few days. For many of us, this is disheartening and might even convince some filmmakers to give up on crowdfunding entirely. I've seen it happen a few times. I've watched campaigns sit through what I call "The Lull" like someone caught in a pit of quicksand. Some panic and sink faster while others simply allow themselves to founder until the days count down to zero.

The same thing happened when I was crowdfunding, and it happened very early on in the campaign. I received a few contributions, sent out a few perks, and then, without warning, an entire day went by without a single contribution. I waited. Then the next day I met with more of the same: not one funder stepped forward. Not a single retweet on Twitter. Not one reply to my email blast. So I did what anyone else in this predicament would do. I panicked, too.

This was a premature reaction, of course. Shortly after, I realized that there's no sense in panicking since it's completely unproductive. I needed a proactive way to deal with this two-day Lull, and that's when I became a lot more playful with my online promotion. I hadn't realized it, but I was doing the same kind of promotion that companies would do to market a product. But crowdfunding for a film is not about products, it's about projects and the people behind them, and you should have as much fun with your fundraising as you would making your film. So I started reaching out and giving my friends and followers a more personal reason to help *Cerise* as contributors or supporters.

Yes, even something like the Lull becomes a question of community engagement. Let's go back to the example of that person stuck in the quicksand. In every movie you can probably think of, it always takes another person to come to the aid of the one who's sinking. That person cannot get out of that predicament by him- or herself. In the case of crowdfunding, amidst a vast desert of campaigns all raising money for various film projects, it's up to you to show the community why *your* film project is worth their support and a little help out from the quicksand.

But you also have to show them that you're not giving up just because a couple of days have passed and none of your followers have seen a "thank you" Tweet or status update welcoming a new contributor into the fold of your film campaign. You have to keep the flow of your campaign moving forward, and sometimes that means changing your approach to it. This hearkens back to the simple genius of Bruce Lee: "Be water" and you'll flow forward. A few rocks in the path of a stream don't stop the stream. The water will find a way around the rocks, slip between the cracks, and keep moving toward its destination.

In the event of a Lull, be creative and innovative, and wake that Lull with promotion that will engage your community. These innovations may not always work, but they will keep the flow of your campaign constant and on the minds of potential contributors and supporters. During the Lull that *Cerise* endured, Marinell and I brainstormed ways to keep our community engaged. We came up with a few interactive ideas, one of which was a "Spelling Twee," a Twitter-based spelling bee in which we'd Tweet an audio link of a word and our followers could then attempt to spell the word out in a Tweet. It kept a few people engaged in between my newly personalized promotion tactics, but did not have the success we thought it would have.

Other ways to stream your way around the rocks of the Lull include contests, giveaways, special incentives, and limited-time perks. Everybody loves to receive things, so if you're constantly promoting and aren't seeing a substantial rise in your funds, set up a contest that's somehow related to your film project. That's sort of what I did with the Spelling Twee. Assuming that the same followers would be playing, whoever got the most words correct would receive a cerise-colored Twibbon, which is a ribbon that you can append to your Twitter avatar to show support for something. Why a Twibbon? It was pretty trendy at the time, and it's always good to keep up with the latest Twitter trends and topics.

You can also hold a contest that is in no way related to your project except for the fact that it may be reserved for contributors only. For instance, during the *Cerise* campaign, Marinell and I held a contest in which we chose a few random Indiegogo funders to receive a DVD copy of one of my previous short films as a way to build up more excitement about *Cerise*, since this was a film people would not find anywhere on the Internet.

Special incentives are another great way to draw more support from your community, especially if it's "for a limited time only." It shows your community that you're going the extra mile to bring in new contributors and get closer to your fundraising goal. With *Cerise*, I didn't need to offer any special incentives during its Indiegogo campaign, but during my Third Crusade for *Cerise*, to rack up the submission fees for some of the final festivals I hoped would accept the film, I offered for a limited time a signed DVD copy of *Cerise*. And that proved incentive enough to get the last few submission fees covered.

The more fun, innovative, and relevant you make your special incentives, however, the faster you'll free your campaign from the Lull. A prime example is Gary King's second Kickstarter campaign for his movie musical *How Do You Write a Joe Schermann Song*. This campaign was all about the music — the main reason for it was to raise $18,000 so that Gary could record a score with a live orchestra. His special incentive at any dollar amount was for the backer to give him a word that he would compile for composer Joe Schermann, who would then work it into the lyrics of a song that he'd compose and the cast of *How Do You Write a Joe Schermann Song* would perform. There are about 150 words on this list — that's 150 backers out of 244 total backers by the end of this second successful campaign.

Although the Lull can seem like a frightening place and maybe even make you feel that crowdfunding isn't for you, it's really just a stepping-stone that can help you think more creatively about your campaign. It may even help you discover new, more innovative ways to go about keeping your community invested enough in your project to help you pull through the dark times and onto the sunlit path ahead.

Chapter Twenty-Five

. . .

BUILD RELATIONSHIPS, NOT TRANSACTIONS

SLAVA RUBIN SAYS IT BEST: "The world is shifting from a world of transactions to a world of relationships." Nowadays, no one wants to be treated like a customer, and I don't think anyone ever did before. When it comes to crowdfunding for your film project, everything you are putting into your campaign — time, money, promotion, Tweets, and status updates — should be grounded firmly in the idea of building relationships as opposed to networks or connections. Not every contributor will be an actual investor in your film project, giving a large sum of money and hoping for a return on their investment, plus a little extra. Some of them will be everyday people contributing to your campaign in exchange for a specific perk. Both types of contributors are key to the future of your film. Therefore, it's important to always give them more, to strive to make them feel more special than just another customer or contributor, and there are a few ways to do this.

One way is to treat your contributors the same way you would treat your actual friends, both online and offline. If certain contributors are fellow filmmakers or artists of other kinds, an easy way to make them feel like they're more than just a person who gave you money for your film is to support them in their own artistic endeavors. That means that if they have a film screening happening in your area, make an effort to attend it. If they're musicians and are about to release a new album, be one of the first to buy or download a copy, and then write a review about it. It's important to reciprocate in some way the support that other artists have shown you during your crowdfunding campaign.

More often than not, once you start crowdfunding, you'll notice that many of the people in your network are also crowdfunding and will support you either financially as a contributor or in other ways. You should demonstrate support for them and their campaigns. It will not only show them that you're a supporter of their work, but that you may be a supporter of their future projects, too. Of course, by ping-ponging support from friend to friend, you build a stronger support system between you and your fellow artists, one that has a very natural flow to it.

There are, however, people who will not necessarily share these sentiments and only be in it for themselves. They may not help you back if you help push them on by showing encouragement for their projects. They may not necessarily contribute to your campaign even though you poured fifty of your hard-earned dollars into their campaign instead of your own. It's unfortunate, but these people do exist, and you will encounter them. The worst thing you can do is succumb to these unpromising circumstances and allow the bad taste to remain in your mouth. One apple does not spoil the bunch. Toss it out and keep on keeping on.

We all know that people have a tendency to judge others by the company they keep. In that sense, we should heed the advice of the ancient Greek philosopher Epictetus, who tells us, "The key is to keep company only with people who uplift you, whose presence calls forth your best." That is also the secret message of *Pu*, the uncarved block. It requires us to let our world and those who come into contact with it mold us into only our very best, much the way our contributors will mold the success of our campaigns by giving money, support, a score, and even a website to our crowdfunding campaigns. All of it will ultimately make our finished films the best they can be.

"When the block is carved, it becomes useful," says Lao Tzu in his *Tao Te Ching*. In that sense, those who help us carve it are responsible for so much more than any simple professional network can bestow. They are friends in the truest sense of the word.

· Part Four ·
SUMMARY POINTS

- Don't solicit (ask). Elicit (evoke).

- Promote strongly through email and on your social networks, but avoid email inundation and social deluge ("The Flood") at all costs.

- With crowdfunding, help can come in various forms, from monetary contributions and investments to donations of music scores, websites, and the many other costly aspects of moviemaking that turn a good film into a great one.

- "The Lull" should be seen as an opportunity to switch up your campaign strategy as opposed to a white flag signaling your surrender.

- Seek to build relationships with every dollar raised; in doing so, you avoid the pitfall of treating contributors and supporters as nothing more than transactions.

· Part Four ·
EXERCISES

1. A little practice in the art of elicitation versus the act of solicitation: Come up with five different ways to write "Please help support this crowdfunding campaign for my film." How might you make people *want* to contribute?

2. Think about your film and its many components, from cinematography to scoring and distribution. What three things would you most like to obtain other than funding for your film project?

3. Let's pretend you've hit "The Lull," perhaps even before your campaign started to really pick up. It may be your pitch — the teaser for your film. Or the fact that your best perk is also your most expensive. Maybe you're flooding your network. How might you not only fix these issues, but also improve upon them?

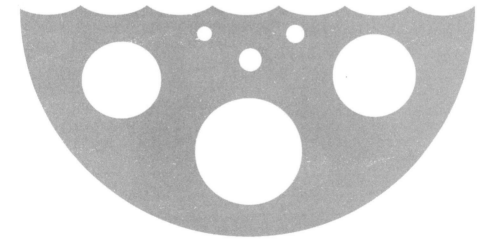

THE TAO OF
TWITTER,
FACEBOOK,
PART
5
AND THE
SOCIAL NETWORK

Chapter Twenty-Six

...

WEI WU WEI: DOING WITHOUT (OVER) DOING

IN VERSE THIRTY-SEVEN of the *Tao Te Ching*, Lao Tzu describes one of the most important principles of Taoism, which is also one of the more difficult to attain, let alone fully understand: "Tao abides in non-action," he begins, "Yet nothing is left undone. / If kings and lords observed this, / The ten thousand things would develop naturally." This is *wu wei* — the principle of non-action.

In today's world, this concept of non-action is even more difficult for many people to fathom. How can anyone get anything done without making an effort to get it done? Without planning ahead? Without strategy or desire? In a crowdfunding sense, there's absolutely no way that your "ten thousand" dollars would be raised if we "kings" and "lords" didn't try to actively raise it.

That's where the key to the Taoist tenet of *wu wei* really lies. Obviously, you should plan ahead and strategize your crowdfunding campaign, and that takes effort. Obviously you should put a fair amount of thought into your pitch, perks, and promotional tactics. And obviously this is what this entire book has been telling you all along. But if you go with the flow of your film project and follow through in your campaign strategy, you avoid overexerting yourself, and that is the real message behind this frequently misinterpreted Taoist principle.

The same is true for when you start promoting your crowdfunding campaign on Facebook, Twitter, and the many other social networking sites on the Internet. You should exercise *wei wu wei*, or action without action. This may seem like a paradox at first glance, but not if you examine it in a slightly larger sense before we dive into its relationship to the microcosm of crowdfunding. Think of it as going with the flow of the social media universe, much like how planets rotate and revolve around the sun. They don't question it. Venus doesn't try and compete with Mars or Earth for the shortest amount of rotations around the sun. The planets simply do what they need to do, and as a result the whole galaxy is kept in balance. It's only when you try and upset that balance that things become difficult and ultimately fall apart.

Back to crowdfunding: you can view the concept of *wei wu wei* as simply knowing when to act and when not to act, specifically in terms of your online promotion. Sometimes we can overdo it and flood our friends' feeds, but oftentimes we allow our own thoughts to dictate whether we'll overdo it *before* ever even doing it. Confused? You're thinking too hard, and thought is the enemy of action. Don't worry — we'll clear up this confusion in these next few chapters, which will show you how to navigate the vast social network without disturbing the universe too much as you inch closer to your goal.

Chapter Twenty-Seven

...

TWITTER TIPS FOR CROWDFUNDERS

IF YOU WERE TRYING to promote your film project in the days before the Internet, you would probably have needed to spend lots of money on print material like flyers, postcards, and business cards to hand out to people. More money spent on those elements meant less money when you completed your fundraising, more physical waste, and more time spent doing something other than making your film. But we're fortunate to live during a time that's made promotion as easy as sending an email or updating one's Facebook status. There's no longer a need to include with your business card a mini CD-ROM showing off your trailer. A potential funder can now simply scan a QR code and watch it right from his or her phone.

Twitter, in particular, has become one of the most powerful tools for marketing your crowdfunding campaign since it forces you to be concise and to think in what's referred to as "Tweetable quotes," which someone else might easily remember, repeat, and ultimately retweet. It's also powerful because of its real-time nature; the second you get news, you can share it right at that moment and it can reach thousands of people within the next minute, if you know how to maximize your reach into the vast Twitterverse.

That said, here are a few tips I've taken away from my own experiences crowdfunding *Cerise* and by keeping a keen eye on other Indiegogo and Kickstarter campaigns that are doing it right.

BE A PROLOGUE BEFORE A PETITION

I joined Twitter on May 4, 2009. I began crowdfunding for *Cerise* on

February 2, 2010, nine months after I had birthed a modest following of about 200 or so Twitter users. The first people I started following were friends, of course. Then I started searching hashtags (#film and #filmmaking at first) and following Twitter handles for people like @gregorybayne and @kingisafink — people who shared interests similar to mine. It wasn't long before I was engaging in meaningful 140-character conversations about obscure directors like Alejandro Jodorowsky and sharing my insights on filmmaking, screenwriting, and storytelling with people who followed my Tweets.

It would later be these same followers who would make up my core of initial funders for *Cerise*. Had I not given myself ample time to genuinely get to know these individuals, to forge actual relationships instead of just networks, I doubt that many of them would have felt a desire to contribute $50 or more to my campaign. People give to people, yes, but do people give to strangers? Yes — you may give a quarter, even a dollar, to the less fortunate, but not $25 or $50. Therefore, you should avoid being misconstrued as someone who has set up a Twitter account for the sole purpose of promoting his or her crowdfunding campaign. Nothing spells S-P-A-M more than that.

CREATIVITY IS KING

Because you've only got 140 characters with which to capture your potential contributors' attention, it's important to be as creative as possible when phrasing your Tweets. It takes a little more time, but your followers will appreciate it. They'll see that you're not a @CampaignBot flooding them with the same Tweet over and over again about your film's campaign, but an actual person who painstakingly crafts each and every promotional Tweet as an affirmation of the passion you feel for it.

Sometimes even the most creative tweeters and retweeters come out with more run-of-the-mill Tweets, like Leilani Holmes's Tweet for *Clowning Around*, which is actually the generic Tweet that Indiegogo sets up for you: "Help make it happen for *Clowning Around* on #Indiegogo." This isn't a very compelling Tweet, truth be told, and even Indiegogo knows this, which is why once you click "Tweet" from its sharing toolbar, everything gets highlighted except the link for easy deleting so you can write your own, more personal message. Kickstarter does the same, so there's no excuse for anyone not to have a little fun with his or her promotion, like crowdfunding champ Gavin Ap'Morrygan (@Tearsinrain78) and supporter Graham Inman (@grahaminman) did here for the same project:

Tearsinrain78 Gavin apmorrygan
Get your tix to the circus RT @grahaminman: Bonzo and a Bottle on Clowning Around on #indiegogo igg.me/p/6492?a=53624...
#clowningaroundfilm
3 Aug

A playful Tweet by @Tearsinrain78 and @grahaminman during the campaign for the short film Clowning Around.

STAY OUT OF "THE LOOP"

Even a quirky Tweet like Gavin and Graham's can lose its charm and freshness if your followers see the same exact Tweet three times in a row from three different people. If you have a personal Twitter account and a separate handle for your film, do your followers a favor and keep them separate. Linking your personal and project accounts can be detrimental to your crowdfunding efforts. People don't like to hear the same things twice, and chances are the majority of your followers are also following your film project. If your accounts are linked, your Tweets will quickly become redundant. It becomes even more perilous to a crowdfunding campaign if you have several members of your team on Twitter and your film project all linked together. Then it becomes spam. Therefore, you should strive to put in the extra effort and make every Tweet from every account something special and worth reading.

Always Include Your (Shortened) Link

Whenever you Tweet about your film campaign, you should always include a link to its homepage so that the first thing a potential contributor sees after he or she clicks the link is your pitch video. Because links can be pretty lengthy at times, and on Twitter, every letter and space is precious, you should always use a link-shortening service like Add This, Bitly, or Owly, which will allow you the freedom to be creative in your Tweets and supply your followers with a link to your campaign.

Add This is a very popular link-shortening service. It's a plug-in that can be used with Firefox and other Internet browsers that allows users to shrink and share a link from a page they're currently viewing. Bitly and Owly are very similar, though Bitly is probably the better of the two. Aside from its excellent tracking capabilities, Bitly also allows its users to customize their links; so, for instance, the link to your film's campaign could read "bitly.com/CeriseIGG," which would bring a potential contributor to *Cerise*'s Indiegogo page. I find this feature particularly useful when Tweeting from a mobile device because it's much easier to remember a customized link while you're on the go as opposed to a string of random letters and numbers, no matter how short. Bitly also generates a QR code, which can be scanned by a mobile device and bring a potential contributor who's particularly techno-savvy right to your campaign's homepage.

There's also Hootlet, which, like Add This, is a plug-in for your browser and allows you to shrink and share a link for a page you're viewing via the Twitter client Hootsuite. The Google Chrome-based web browser RockMelt has similar features for maximizing your Twitter output as well, and rounds out my top five link shorteners.

#Hashtag #Everything #Relevant to Your #Project

In every Tweet you send, be sure to hashtag words and phrases related to your project and campaign. This makes it easy for random people far from your own following to find your project on Twitter or through a Google search. Here's a great example from Meg Pinsonneault's documentary *Gwapa (Beautiful)*:

ThirstyGirlFilm Meg Pinsonneault
#GwapaFilm is 22% funded with just 10 days left! Get involved with a great project & #HelpSaveLives! #documentary #kids
indiegogo.com/Gwapa-Film
2 hours ago

Meg Pinsonneault's Tweet for Gwapa (Beautiful) *makes excellent use of hashtags to reach out to various audiences.*

Right away, I know that this is a #documentary about #kids, and there's an urgency to #HelpSaveLives. Meg and her team also switched up their hashtags each time they Tweeted about #GwapaFilm; some Tweets will highlight #Filipino, since this is a documentary about helping the children of two Filipino families who have cleft lip or cleft palate. Other Tweets focused on the film's #inspirational nature.

The first thing you'll want to do is to find out what words or phrases relevant to your film bring specific communities together on Twitter. Think of these as little galaxies in a vast cosmos of galaxies. The easiest way to find a specific community is to plug in the coordinates (hashtags) into your "navicomputer" and you'll reach your destination. For making movies, I've found that #film, #indiefilm, #supportindiefilm, and #filmmaking are all popular hashtags for connecting to these communities. If you're raising money for a short film about an underdog who becomes a king in a fantasy world, I would hashtag all of the above, plus #fantasy and #underdog for direct access to those groups, as well as #sci-fi and #shortfilm to indirectly make your way into related communities.

REMEMBER — DON'T SOLICIT, ELICIT

I introduced this "Golden Rule" back in Chapter Twenty, and I've included it as a Twitter tip as well because this is doubly true when using this particular social network. Simply asking people to visit your Indiegogo or Kickstarter page will only get you so far in your campaign, and it may even get you all the way to your crowdfunding goal. But if your aim is to raise upward of $10,000, you'll most likely need to expand your network. The way to do that is to start eliciting responses from potential contributors and supporters if you want to bring in larger contributions and a handful of retweets from your network that are more personal than a click of the retweet button.

Here's an example of a Tweet that solicits, or asks, for help, from filmmaker Will Warner for his web series: "Please help me to fund my next film *Tales of the Black Ghost.*" Again, there's nothing wrong with a Tweet like this, of course, but it's too similar to the typical "Make it happen for (fill in your campaign here)" Indiegogo Tweet. Now look at this Tweet from Wonder Russell that elicits, or evokes a response: "A small town pizza girl. Gary Busey. Seattle Indie. Let's Finish *Jenny.*"

Obviously, this Tweet for finishing funds for Sam Graydon's *Jenny* is meant to intrigue and make you want to click the link to see what this campaign is all about. So as much as possible throughout your crowdfunding campaign, elicit responses from your followers because you'll more than likely elicit something more tangible than a $10 or $100 contribution.

PEOPLE NEED THEIR SPACE

As with most social networking sites, Twitter has undergone some major upgrades, some of which are real assets while others serve only to upset its users to no end. One of those changes was the advent of the retweet button, which is a simple one-click answer to retweeting something you enjoyed reading on Twitter and felt the urge to share. But many people still prefer the previous method of retweeting, which is to append their own messages before an "RT" and as much of the original message as possible. Twitter now calls this "Quote Tweet" and adds quotation marks around the original Tweet.

Keeping this difference in mind, if by the time you click "Send" your character count is already at zero, you risk possibly losing a more personalized, ardently-expressed retweet from a supporter who perhaps, through his or her words, could elicit a contribution from some of his or her followers. Twitter is about concision — saying things the shortest way possible. Chilean director Alejandro Jodorowsky once said during an interview that "Twitter is the haiku of our century." If that's true, or if you've ever tried to write a haiku, it's safe to say it's the most difficult thing to write. The shorter, the better, especially if you're going to rely on others to help spread the word about your campaign. If you make them work too hard, or force them to think too hard about which of your words to omit so they can squeeze in some of theirs, they'll eventually give up the fight and reach for the retweet button.

A well-crafted Tweet is no accident, but remember to keep it short and simple and leave at least fifteen characters available for that super-passionate backer to RT with ease.

@Everybody

Whenever you thank a contributor, be sure to mention (@) that person on Twitter. If you're not sure if he or she has a Twitter account or don't know that person's handle, do a quick Google search of that person's name and "on Twitter" and you'll probably find him or her fairly easy. Even if the person you're thanking doesn't sign in to Twitter very often or even if his or her little pastel egg of a profile picture hasn't hatched into the person you know and follow, you should show your appreciation as a campaigner nonetheless so it's on the record, transparent and in plain sight of everyone.

Make Things Easier with a Twitter Client

I mentioned a few of these in the section about link shorteners, but if Twitter is going to be a train on which a hefty amount of your promotion will ride, then I recommend making your life easier by working with a Twitter client, which is basically an app that makes Tweeting a cinch. Some of the more popular ones include Hootsuite and Tweetdeck, which are relatively the same. I make use of the Twitter app for both my desktop Tweeting and Tweeting from my iPhone.

I also use Tweetdeck and Hootsuite on occasion for different purposes. For instance, I have my Tweetdeck set up with columns that list different hashtags so that I can follow specific crowdfunding projects with ease. One of my columns is for "#Crowdfunding #Indiegogo" and another is for "#SupportIndieFilm." Sometimes I'll list a specific project's campaign, such as "#GwapaFilm" so I can follow all the Tweets that mention that hashtag or phrase and keep up to date with all that's going on with those projects.

Perhaps the most convenient aspect of any Twitter client is the ability to schedule Tweets, which can make crowdfunding a bit less stressful. If you know you have a full day of work ahead of you at the day job, you can schedule some Tweets about your film's campaign the night before. This way, through the course of the day, you will still appear to be Tweeting and promoting your campaign. But beware: scheduled Tweets should follow the same rules previously mentioned, otherwise, you may stumble into the realm of the @ SpamBot, and your followers may start to ignore your campaigning efforts or unfollow you completely. So schedule Tweets that vary from one to the other, and check your mentions so you can reply to anyone who mentions you or your campaign. This way you give the impression that you are there, giving your all to the campaign trail.

That said, your presence on Twitter as a crowdfunder is really all about personalization. You should be sure to maintain a steady presence on Twitter while you're campaigning by interacting with your followers in ways unrelated to your #Project. Again, people give to people, not bots. Once you nurture and maintain those relationships as a person and a crowdfunder, you will build a network that will walk beside a person they'll be proud to know and support in the future.

Chapter Twenty-Eight

• • •

FROM FACEBOOK PAGES
TO "FRIEND FAWNING"

FACEBOOK, LIKE TWITTER, can be a valuable tool for film-makers crowdfunding their film projects. Like Twitter, you can up-date your status to reflect what you're doing at the moment you're doing it. You can also post photos and videos, "Like" other people's statuses, "Share" something you find interesting with your friends, or post directly to a friend's wall. You can create photo albums so you will always remember your most important life events. You can even "Poke" people to remind them that you're there, though this trend is slowly going out of vogue.

In early 2012, Facebook unveiled Timeline, which has revolution-ized the way people interact with their social network. Split into two columns with a timeline separating them, your status updates and other posts are more easily viewed. What makes Timeline really interesting is the fact that you and your network can easily travel back to a specific month and year and see what you posted back then. More so, Facebook allows you the opportunity to add "Life Events" and other updates to your Timeline as well. In a sense, Facebook is now a complete record of your digital life, organized and at your fingertips. The same has been done for Facebook pages for films, bands, businesses, and organizations.

These are all aspects of Facebook that you'll want to learn about as in-depth as possible so you can maximize how far your film campaign is reaching into Interspace. Aside from simply updat-ing statuses and posting content relevant to your crowdfunding campaign, there are a few other helpful things you may want to consider. You can set up a Facebook page for your film project, a Facebook event, Facebook Messages, and a somewhat controversial tactic I've affectionately termed "Friend Fawning."

FACEBOOK PAGES

Setting up a Facebook page for your film or video project is simple enough, but before you jump into filling in all the pertinent details about your project, you may want to make certain of two key things: First, that you have time to update your film's Facebook page, and second, that you have content with which to update the page. I mention these because there's a difference between engagement, maintenance, and stagnation. The latter won't help you with your crowdfunding campaign in any way if your film's page is lifelessly collecting e-dust. Maintenance usually means updating a status once a day or posting a photo every week or two, but this will give people little reason to "Like" your page. Engagement, on the other hand, will show that things are moving forward, which will also boost your social proof, having friends and those who "Like" your film's page actively participate in its success.

Once you've finished the initial steps of setting up your Facebook page and have added a profile pic and some basic information like a synopsis, website URL, and a list of the people responsible for your film, it's time to build awareness of your page. One way is to make it easy for people to "Like" your film's Facebook page from your film's Indiegogo or Kickstarter home page or your personal or movie's website. This can be done right on your "Get Started" page by clicking "Add Like Box" under "Promote This Page on Your Website." Yes, this means people will already have to know about your film's campaign, but the whole purpose of the Facebook page should be to build further awareness of the film, not necessarily your crowdfunding campaign.

Another way to get word out quickly about your film's Facebook page is to link your Facebook page's updates to Twitter. Now you might be thinking to yourself, *But didn't you just tell me in the previous chapter not to connect your Twitter and Facebook accounts?!* Yes, I did. But with your Facebook page, it's a bit different. If you connect your personal Facebook page with your movie's Twitter account, for instance, every single update you post will be a Tweet, whether or not it's related to your film and/or campaign. If you're posting as *Sync the Movie* on Facebook, however, and the corresponding Tweet is being sent out from @SyncMovie, that's marketing. But if your Facebook page and Twitter account are also linked to your personal page or Twitter account, then it becomes spam of the first magnitude and should be avoided.

One of the only snags with linking your film's Facebook and Twitter accounts is that you'll ultimately blur the invisible line between these two diverse social networks. Hashtags and mentions are exclusive to Twitter, but you'll have to include them in your status updates if you want them to appear on Twitter. You can also post additional Tweets directly from Twitter that include hashtags and mentions, but if you're in a pinch for time, doing it from Facebook will save some valuable minutes. My suggestion, however, is to Tweet a Tweet, update a Facebook status, and keep them separate, if time permits, of course.

How does having a Facebook page up and active during your film's crowdfunding campaign benefit your efforts? Most importantly, it will build up your audience and draw in new potential contributors to your campaign. If they visit the page and give it a "Like," then discover from a status update that you're crowdfunding on Kickstarter for funding, they may click the link to your campaign, which for the time being should be listed as your film's website as well, and contribute a few dollars to a film that they "Like" and would probably enjoy watching in the future.

Cerise is an interesting exception with regard to its Facebook page. My team and I didn't have one until after the film was shot and in the editing room, mainly because crowdfunding for three months was time-consuming enough for us without having to worry about updating our own Facebook accounts *and* the movie's page. If you feel that it may be too much, you can opt to start your film's page after crowdfunding is complete. If you have someone who can take care of those updates for you, then an active Facebook page while crowdfunding can only enhance your outreach and attract even more potential contributors to your crowdfunding campaign.

For more information on how to get the most out of your Facebook page, you should "Like" and peruse Facebook Pages, which offers a full set of links covering things like advertising on Facebook, social plug-ins such as the "Like" button and comments, and even a helpful section titled "Best Practices to Marketing on Facebook." But remember to always keep your personal touch touching others. This is your film we're talking about marketing, not a real estate agency.

FACEBOOK EVENTS

Many crowdfunders set up a Facebook event to further build awareness for their campaign. At the top of a Facebook event is where all the pertinent information should be. In an event titled "Help Me Change Lives!" for the film *Gwapa* (*Beautiful*), Meg Pinsonneault included the dates for the event. The location is "At your computer!" (Traditionally, Facebook events started out as exclusively physical ones, in which you'd put a location, but for a crowdfunding event such as this, you can be fun with the location, like Meg, so long as people know that there's no actual location.) Following all this is a more detailed description of the event.

The one thing I would critique about Meg's description is that there is no spot for the Indiegogo link, and that should be somewhere before the "See more" link we'd have to click to find out where to go to contribute. I strongly suggest putting the website URL in the location field, since that's where the crowdfunding event is taking place, much how Internet radio host Nic Baisley did with his "Film Snobbery's Moving to LA! — An Indiegogo Campaign" Facebook event, which brought potential contributors to his page much more efficiently and with fewer clicks.

Between pages and events, the question becomes how much time can you realistically allot to your Facebook promotion during your crowdfunding campaign? If the answer is "not much," then I suggest setting up a Facebook event for your campaign and leave the Facebook page for later, once your film is shot and ready for editing. If you can do both and keep your friends — those who are "Going" to your event and those who "Like" your page — engaged with fresh content on a regular basis, then you'll be raising a profound awareness of and urgency for your campaign, as well as an anticipation for people to see the finished product.

Facebook Messages

Another way to spread the word about your film campaign on Facebook is to send messages to your friends. This is the same as an email blast, and since this is the case, you'll definitely get both positive and not-so-positive results. One of my friends used a Facebook message to beckon me to "Stop sending these messages!!" This will happen if you send more than two messages, but out of my 300 or so friends at the time, I lost that one and gained over 600. The general rule should be this: If the majority of your friends ask you to stop, you should stop; but if it's just one or a few, it's simply marketing. You can probably spare the loss of those couple of friends without shedding too many tears.

Since my time crowdfunding *Cerise*, though, Facebook messages have evolved and now allow people to "Leave" conversations they don't want to be a part of, a very positive step forward since now there's no unfriending needed. If they tire of seeing their feed bombarded with promotions and links for your film campaign, they can now uncheck "Show in News Feed" rather than unfriend you. This way you stay friends but you won't appear in their feed anymore. When sending messages to your friends on Facebook, you should be concise and only include the basics of what they need to know in order to show their support, which is the link to your campaign's home page and a good reason to support you. Aside from that, everything else in a message is irrelevant.

A good practice is to create a Facebook event and send a very short and sweet message to your friends on Facebook letting them know about your event and, if you've set one up, your film's page on Facebook. This way, they get the message, as sometimes people don't check their "Events" tab as often as we crowdfunders would hope. Also, you'll get more people "Going" without having to worry about offending anyone with a long-winded message asking them for money even though you haven't spoken to them since high school.

That said, one thing you should try your best to do is only send messages to the people with whom you are fairly active on Facebook. No one likes to add someone because he or she seems interesting, and then two or three days later get a message about a project and how this new friend needs help financing it. Again, it's about relationships and building them up into a powerful social network. A friend request is a virtual handshake, and the first time you shake hands with someone, you wouldn't ask that person to buy you a drink. The same rule applies here. You need to get to know some of these people, "Like" some of their status updates, and occasionally comment on their posts. If their updates are interesting, you may want to follow them on Twitter, as well. Show them that you're making an effort to get to know them on a deeper digital level.

Ever since crowdfunding *Cerise*, I've gained a lot of friends on Facebook. Similarly, whenever I start helping filmmakers who are crowdfunding, I receive a surplus of friend requests, and I make it a point to send short hello messages thanking each person for his or her request. I also check out a new friend's page to see what we've got in common and reference it in my message, so that my new friend knows I took some time to get to know who he or she is before accepting the friend request. Crowdfunding is about building bridges, one message at a time.

Friend Fawning

This brings us to the final approach to really bringing in the contributions to your crowdfunding campaign via Facebook, but this one is not for the faint of heart. In fact, out of *Cerise*'s modest team of three, I was the only one who felt comfortable enough doing this without worrying about how many friends I might lose in the process. No one, no matter how devout they are about filmmaking, will be as passionate and no-holds-barred about your film project as you are.

This tactic was spawned during *Cerise*'s second "Lull." I hadn't been getting many responses from my Facebook messages except for that one ex-friend who asked me to stop, and I suddenly got nervous that my crowdfunding efforts so far were all for naught. But as with everything else regarding filmmaking and life, it's not about quitting, it's about figuring out new ways to approach a problem and deal with it. I didn't know how this particular solution would affect my Facebook friendships, but I decided to risk it because I believed that strongly in my project.

That said, I introduce to you a Facebook device (though it can be used with Google Plus and any other Facebook-style social networking sites) I've called "Friend Fawning," which is basically writing directly on your individual friends' walls about your crowdfunding campaign. At first, this may seem invasive — it's one thing to post a YouTube video that you found enjoyable and thought your friend might find it so, too; it's quite another to post a link to your Indiegogo campaign on his or her wall for not only him or her, but for that person's friends to see as well. But as I learned, it's all about how you present yourself and your campaign.

As I mentioned in the section on Facebook messages, you shouldn't ever message random strangers for money. You have to form a connection fairly quickly in a single wall post. I find this to be a threefold process, much like recording your pitch video: there's the *greeting*, followed by the *personal touch*, and finally, the *pitch*. For *Cerise*, I started out with a standard greeting like, "Hey Jim, it's been a while, huh?" I like to start with a question because I find most people will respond to something that's asked rather than a statement like, "It's been way too long!" Then, I'd find something on their page that I could mention to show that I've been keeping up with their lives, even though at the time it may not have been entirely true. Usually, this was something related to one of their latest status updates, and it would be something like, "I can't believe your son's walking already — That's awesome!"

Then comes the pitch. This requires a smooth transition from the personal touch — which is all about your friend — to the pitch, which is all about you and your project. Perhaps transition with something along the lines of, "I know you've got your hands full with your family, but… " and then dive into a concise pitch: "… I'm raising funds for my next film and I'd really appreciate if you could help out with $5. Check out my page." Then, of course, include the link to your crowdfunding campaign's home page.

Occasionally, I'd put a very low dollar amount like $5, and most people would contribute at least $10 since that was the starting contribution. Sometimes I wouldn't put any dollar amount, and instead I would simply tell them "there are a lot of cool perks for different dollar amounts." Other times, I would highlight the most personal perk for *Cerise*, which was the acrostic poem, and leave it at that. These frequent change-ups of the wording will keep your wall posts from registering on your friends' radars as spam, as well as show that there's an actual person behind each post.

There will be some friends who will not answer these wall posts at all. There'll even be some who delete it. But many will respond because people value the friendships they have on Facebook, especially if you're friends outside of Facebook. Others may answer because they might be wondering things like *how long has this post been on my wall?* and *how many of my friends have seen this post already?* They won't want to look bad to their friends if they refuse to reply in some way to your post.

How often should you fawn your friends on Facebook? I follow the rule of three in just about everything, and this is no different. If I posted about *Cerise* one week, I waited about five days before I posted another message and link on the same person's wall. If that person didn't reply to it by then, I waited a full week and posted once more. After a third time and still no reply, I figured he or she didn't want to be bothered by me or my project, or he or she'd unfriended or even blocked me by then, which is essentially the same. At least with *Cerise*, I very rarely had to fawn the same friend more than once, and I was very happy with the contributions that amounted due to this tactic. Some friends gave $10, but many gave a minimum of $50, which really helped get me to my goal much faster.

It seems like a lot of work at first glance, but in all honesty, it's not, if you've got your eye on the prize — the target goal for your crowdfunding campaign. In terms of *wei wu wei*, this is really doing without doing. If we're a part of a social network like Facebook, and we're viewing our friends' status updates, that means we want to know what these friends are up to. In this sense, you're simply going with the flow and interacting with your friends — the primary difference being you have a stronger reason to interact. As controversial as it may seem to some, it's because of friend fawning that I've taken a more genuine interest in everything that my friends are posting on Facebook, and I now make sure to take a few minutes out of every day to keep updated on film projects, family milestones, and recent photos and videos.

We are all part of a community, after all.

Chapter Twenty-Nine

• • •

SLEEP STRIKES, TWEETATHONS, AND OTHER LAST-MINUTE STRATEGIES

AS THE CROWDFUNDING CAMPAIGN for your film project presses on into its final days and hours, if you are less than 50% funded, chances are one of two things will happen: either you'll give up the fight entirely, or you'll push on and take some drastic measures to ensure you reach your crowdfunding goal. While giving up is understandable under certain circumstances, it really isn't an option since it will show your contributors that you didn't believe that strongly in your film project, and it'll be a tough task to regain the trust of those contributors if and when you crowdfund your next film project. I've seen campaign owners give up days before their campaigns had ended, and I've even seen others cancel their fundraising altogether.

People will always root for the underdog, but an underdog isn't someone who is lackadaisical. Laziness throughout the duration of our campaigns doesn't make us underdogs in the eyes of potential contributors — it makes us lazy. There are so many reasons why a campaign sometimes can't take off, and in the end, if the person shows him- or herself to be industrious, diligent, and willing to do whatever it takes to make his or her film a reality, the community will see this and come together to make it happen. But in this case, there is no *wu wei*, there's only *wei* — doing.

The following strategies are a few of the more popular last-minute approaches to crowdfunding that will demonstrate to potential contributors how serious you still are about your film project and campaign despite the odds that may now be piled up against you. These tactics will also serve to spark in your Facebook friends, Twitter followers, and current and potential contributors some added excitement, and just like watching a nail-biting thriller, you'll want to keep them thinking one question: *How's it going to end?*

TWEETATHONS

If you append a "Tw-" before just about any word, it automatically becomes something specifically for Twitter. Twibbon. Spelling Twee. Twitterverse. So, naturally, a marathon of Tweets is a Tweetathon. A tweetathon may also have its roots in the word "telethon," a TV program typically held to raise money for a specific cause. Therefore, a tweetathon is a telethon of constant Tweets about your crowdfunding campaign. But the heart of a tweetathon lies in the duration — it will be lengthy.

A tweetathon doesn't necessarily have to be used as a last-minute tactic, of course. I've seen tweetathons set up at the beginning and middle of campaigns, and for a limited time. Take A. D. Lane's independent crowdfunding campaign for *Invasion of the Not Quite Dead*. Lane's been running his signature "non-stop tweetathons" since May 2009. If you're like Lane, you don't necessarily have to mention that you're running a tweetathon. All you need to do is to Tweet intensely for a certain amount of time and squeeze a few personal Tweets into the mix to break up the inevitable monotony that even the most personalized, creative Tweets will suffer from. On the other hand, announcing a tweetathon can be smart since it gives the sense that it will be for a limited time only or until a certain amount is reached.

SLEEP STRIKES

Perhaps nothing is more fun than staying up all hours of the night with a hot cup of cocoa and Twitter lighting up your Internet browser as you Tweet with friends about your crowdfunding campaign and various other topics. If one person does this by him- or herself, we might think this person takes social networking a bit too seriously. But when you have a group of people all vowing to stay up until a certain dollar amount is met, you now have a sleep strike, a very useful tactic in the battle to raise funds from the crowd.

It usually starts with a single 140-character call to action, something along the lines of "Sleep strike until #YourFilm reaches $5K." Then, some of your strongest supporters will join in with retweets or their own personalized Tweets. This will go on for hours until the designated amount is raised or until each and everyone falls asleep because of sheer exhaustion, but not for lack of trying to keep their eyelids open and their fingers Tweeting.

A sleep strike is no light matter, however. The human body can only take so much before it starts shutting itself down despite your own will to continue. But the power of the sleep strike lies in the fact that not only the project owner but also other people out in the Twitter-verse are all coming together to bring a campaign to the next level. Some people will only last a few hours. Some can go a day or two. If you attempt this and then eventually go quiet, one of the other sleep strikers may check on you with a Tweet, since if the project owner falls asleep, all is lost.

LAST-MINUTE PERKS

Sometimes your current perks are just not enough to push you over the last hump of funding you need to obtain a crowdfunding victory, especially when the clock is counting down the final minutes of your indie film campaign. At this point, it may take a little more than that signed postcard at the $10 level to get you $30,000 and up.

As an added incentive to entice potential contributors to come to the aid of your film campaign as it races toward the finish line, come up with one or two new, limited-edition perks. Take the Kickstarter campaign for *Crowned*, a web series about party princesses by Josh Bednarsky and Brianne Sanborn, which raised $328 over its goal of $8,000. But toward the end, they weren't certain they'd make it. I suggested to Josh that he come up with some last-minute perks to offer potential contributors. Shortly after, he announced a pair of new perks on Twitter. One included a limited-edition T-shirt, a mention in their behind-the-scenes video, and a thank you card signed by the cast and crew for a pledge of $30. The last-minute perk that made the difference was Josh's offering a co-producer credit on the film's IMDb page, as well as the backer's name in the film, for a pledge of $375. Considering that to be a producer a backer would need to contribute $1,000 to *Crowned*, a co-producer credit at just under $400 is a steal and raked in some additional funding to help them up and over their goal.

Another option, and oftentimes just as effective, is to do a little rearranging of your current perks. Maybe you have a really cool perk at the $500 level, but no one's choosing it because it may be set at too high an amount. Why not offer that perk at a lower amount, say $250 or even $100, for a limited time? Or temporarily move the executive producer credit you've been offering at $1,000 to the $500 tier and see how many new executive producers you welcome to the fold. Of course, you would need to sound the trumpets about these limited-time perks on your social networks to draw the most attention to it, and by doing so, you'll most likely see a sharp rise in your campaign activity. This can mean the difference between a victory and a near miss, especially when it's all or nothing.

One thing's for sure, though: Whatever last-minute perks you introduce to your campaign during the final hours and minutes, they've got to be good! Remember, people look for connections between projects and their perks. When you're under the all-or-nothing gun, you've got to show people how much of yourself you're willing to give them for their immediate support of your film project.

Chapter Thirty

• • •

A Few Should-Nots
of Crowdfunding

TAOISM IS ABOUT FINDING the positive in everything and nurturing it to benefit you and the world around you. The same holds true with crowdfunding. So far I've been focusing on the positive things that filmmakers should do to successfully crowdfund their film projects, but balance dictates that where there's a positive, there's also a negative, or else the former couldn't exist. When promoting our campaigns heavily on our social networks, we constantly run the risk of going overboard and falling off the tightrope into the dark side of promotion: spam.

The following are a few do-nots of crowdfunding, or rather a few should-nots, since doing them won't automatically excommunicate you from your indie film and crowdfunding circles. These are some things you should avoid simply to keep the experience of crowdfunding positive for you, your potential contributors, and your most ardent supporters.

Facebook Groups

Facebook has a surplus of valuable tools for crowdfunders to use, such as messages, events, and pages. There are also groups, in which you can add specific people you want to communicate with and indulge in conversations with more ease than by chatting, sending messages, or even emailing. This works fine for film groups and companies, but setting up a group for your crowdfunding campaign may lead to overkill, especially if most of your supporters and contributors are now your Facebook friends and/or have liked your film's Facebook page. In this way, updates can quickly become redundant, since you already have a sufficient number of ways to interact with your contributors via your crowdfunding platform, email, Facebook, and Twitter.

"FRIEND FOULING"

Continuing with Facebook, as mentioned in Chapter Twenty-Eight, my "Friend Fawning" tactic, in which you post your link directly onto your friends' walls, is questionable at best, but there's a difference between "Friend Fawning" and "Friend Fouling." The difference is simple: Posting only a link to your crowdfunding campaign on your friend's page can be construed as rude, especially if you haven't spoken to this friend in quite a while or if you've only recently become friends on Facebook. You don't want to purposely foul up your friendships, especially before you nurture them into a trusted network.

EXECUTIVE PRODUCER: A(NOTHER) CROWDFUNDER HAS SENT YOU A FRIEND REQUEST

This one's a biggie. So big I'm using the words "do not" to show how big a point this is. And yes, it does happen, and yes, people do get offended. Obviously you're not going to be the only person in the indie film community who will be crowdfunding for a film project, so naturally you'll be keeping an eye on the campaigns of others. If you see that someone has contributed a substantial amount of money to a single campaign and thus has become an executive producer, as much as you may want to, you really shouldn't send that person a friend request right away. First of all, once that contributor checks you out, he or she'll quickly discover that you are also currently crowdfunding for a film project and may jump to the (correct) conclusion that you're adding him or her in the hopes that he or she might contribute a similar amount to your campaign. That's bad practice in any arena.

This actually did happen. A friend of mine who was crowdfunding for his indie romantic comedy noticed that a few people had contributed to *Cerise*, so he sent them a friend request on Facebook right away. Since I make a point to talk with my funders on a regular basis, a couple of them asked me if I knew this person. Once I asked why, they mentioned that he added them as a friend, but they saw that he was crowdfunding as well and unfriended him. They felt that it was a bit shady of that person to try and jump on the funding bandwagon while the money they gave to *Cerise* was still hot from their pockets.

The only exception might be if the person who contributed the substantial amount is an investor seeking to put money into film projects with the intention of making a return on his or her investment plus some profit. However, many of the everyday people who will give money to a campaign do so because they like the person, the project, or the perks. As a filmmaker, you have to prove that you and/or your film project are worth the contribution, and a surefire way to negate your worth is to friend or start following someone with the sole intention of snatching a contribution in the near future. This practice will not make you or your project sit well with anyone.

Remember: It's Called Promotion, Not Spamotion

Much the same way you shouldn't set up your crowdfunding campaign and let it languish until potential contributors happen upon your film project, you shouldn't assail your friends and supporters with unrelenting activity. You should always strive to be a pro when planning out the promotional tactics for your campaign to avoid the pitfalls of those annoying "Need Cash Now?" advertisements that are texted to people's phones. In the past, when a telemarketer foisted their unfortunate phone calls upon us, we would simply hang up until they got the message. Since the dawn of Facebook and Twitter, such an annoyance is swiftly resolved by clicking the "unfriend" or "unfollow" buttons, and in that moment, you lose not only a friend or follower, but also a supporter, another possible "Like" on your film's Facebook page, or one less subscriber to your YouTube channel. When you disturb the universe, it seeks to balance itself once more, and it will be balanced at the expense of your film project. There's a fine line between promotion and spamotion. There's an even finer line between marketing and desperation.

Since you must promote your film campaign, you should always strive to remain personable in your publicity, and by doing so you steer clear of those dastardly "Report Spam" and "Block" features that get plenty of use on our social networks. Do this, and you'll see firsthand that the personal touch most often leads to the Midas touch.

· PART FIVE ·
SUMMARY POINTS

- *Wei wu wei* is the Taoist principle of non-action, literally "doing without doing." In a crowdfunding sense, this can be translated to doing without *over*doing.

- With promotion on Twitter, there are a few important things to remember, such as always including a shortened link to your campaign's homepage, hashtagging everything relevant to your film, and, of course, eliciting rather than soliciting.

- Facebook has plenty of helpful tools crowdfunders can use to get the word out about their film projects, including pages, events, and messages.

- "Friend Fawning," a controversial tactic primarily used on Facebook, can be made less controversial by including a greeting, personal touch, and then a pitch in every message you post directly onto a friend's wall.

- Amongst some of the crowdfunding should-nots are Facebook groups, "Friend Fouling" (posting only the link to your campaign on someone's wall), and adding executive producers because they gave a substantial amount to another project.

· PART FIVE ·
EXERCISE

"Friend Fawning" vs. "Friend Fouling" — Write up three mock wall posts. Be sure to include the following:

(1) a warm greeting;

(2) a personal touch, something specific about the friend that shows you've been keeping up with his or her Facebook feed;

(3) a smooth transition to

(4) a pitch that elicits that friend's support and a contribution; and

(5) the link to your campaign's home page.

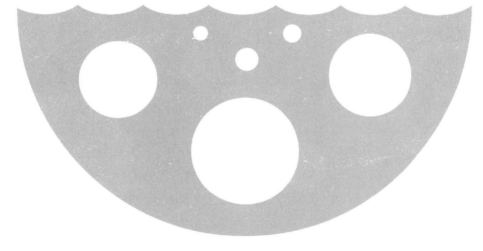

PART 6 ADVANCED CROWDFUNDING

Chapter Thirty-One

...

FROM LAO TZU TO SUN TZU: WAGING THE WAR OF ART

SO FAR, WE'VE GONE DOWN THE LIST from crowdfunding basics to marketing your film's campaign on the social networks. We've even worked in some major tenets of Taoism, demonstrating how, by going with the flow of crowdfunding, your campaign will thrive; how through *Tao* you can set your campaign up with a solid team, the right platform, a tight strategy, and sufficient time to meet and possibly exceed your goal; how through *Te* you'll be able to show to your potential contributors an intimate part of you and your film project in your pitch video, perks, and promotion; how your community can help you shape the *Pu* of your campaign and help carry it toward the finish line; and how the principle of *wu wei* means that you have to get social to make the "ten thousand things," or $10,000 in this case, flow toward you without overdoing your efforts.

These precepts of Taoism are exemplary for launching a successful campaign for your film if you're looking to raise $1,000 to $5,000. You may even be able to secure as much as $10,000 or $15,000. But for a feature-length film that may run up around $30,000 or even $100,000? For that, you'll need to temporarily close the *Tao Te Ching* and unlock the more proactive advice found in one of the world's oldest books on military strategy: Sun Tzu's *The Art of War*.

While everything you've learned about Lao Tzu's Taoist text should still be applied to a crowdfunding campaign attempting to raise $100,000, to even get close to that amount, you'll have to be a bit more active than the Taoist principle of *wu wei* dictates. You may need to crowdfund for a full three months rather than a few weeks.

You may need to lure in larger contributions from individuals and investors who are trying to build a reputation in the industry as an executive or associate producer by giving them added incentives for contributing. You may also need to think about the bigger picture with regard to your film — what's commonly referred to today as *transmedia storytelling* (see Chapter Thirty-Seven) — and attempt to sell people not only on your film, but the larger story it's based around.

Doing this will require running your campaign much the same way an army general might run his campaign, with more strict regimentation than usual. That's where Sun Tzu's war-waging handbook comes into play. In the next chapters, I'll be making a few references to select sections of *The Art of War* that demonstrate how we as crowdfunders have to rethink the *Tao* of crowdfunding to counterbalance our efforts toward more ambitious fundraising goals, and maybe even come out with more than we thought we would once those goals are reached.

Chapter Thirty-Two

• • •

$30,000+ Budgets — How Do They Raise It?

IT TOOK ME TWO SOLID MONTHS of non-stop crowdfunding to reach my goal of $5,000 for my short film *Cerise*. While many DIY filmmakers can make magic with a $15,000 budget, those who want to pursue bigger dreams may need upward of $30,000 both to make a feature-length film that will look and sound the way a movie should, and also market and distribute that film in a way that maximizes the amount of eyes that fall upon it.

For these film projects, you should take everything we've previously learned and amplify it with additional elements that will help strengthen your campaign. The ancient Chinese militarist Sun Tzu was all about prowess and playing the war game smartly. Raising $30,000 to $100,000 and up is a war for your art. At this level, your focus is on laying plans and executing them, because the life of your film project hangs in the balance.

Examining the plans of attack of a small handful of Kickstarter campaigns that have garnered much praise for their crowdfunding strategies in reaching goals between $30,000 and even upward of $300,000, here are a handful of things "you gotta have" in place before marching onto the battlefield.

You Gotta Have a Gimmick

The word "gimmick" tends to get a bad rap. People who sense a gimmick usually back away from a person who's got one. They have a misconception about the word and often confuse it with the word "catch," as in the phrase, "What's the catch?" But a gimmick is really something that calls attention to something else, and if you're crowd-funding for your film project in the hopes of raising $30,000, you're going to need something more than hope and hard work — you're going to *need* a gimmick.

Take Ryan Koo's monumental Kickstarter campaign for *Man-Child*. At first look, Koo's pitch video does all the things a pitch video should do — it's personal, it presents not only the story of *Man-Child*, but also highlights Koo's prior work and awards, and mentions the perks backers will receive for their contributions. But if you're not into basketball or sports movies and you're not into simply help-ing out a young, talented filmmaker struggling to make his first fea-ture film, then this pitch could fall on deaf ears. But Koo also has a gimmick. While his perks aren't very personal and range from DVD copies to a digital download of the film's soundtrack, Koo offers you the individual frames that you as a backer helped make possible.

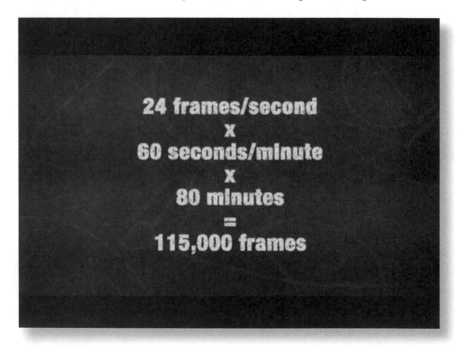

A frame from Ryan Koo's pitch video for Man-Child *explaining his "$1/Frame" perk.*

If you backed *Man-Child* at the $5 level, you'll receive the five frames you helped make possible. If you contributed $24, you get a full one-second clip. Now, while this may not seem like a lot (can you actually watch five frames?), and while it's not personal in any way, Koo's $1 per frame gimmick is certainly interesting enough to make someone contribute, or at the very least prompt him or her to take notice of the project without being a fan of films like *Friday Night Lights* and *Moneyball*.

Another example of a more natural gimmick is Jennifer Fox's campaign for her feature-length documentary *My Reincarnation* about a Tibetan Buddhist master and his son as they tour the world, which raised $150,456 on Kickstarter. This is an example of a campaign strategy that doesn't exactly follow the suggestions mentioned in this book, but it has a gimmick — *My Reincarnation* is "an epic twenty-year journey," and Jennifer herself has been filming for two decades, as she made sure to mention in her description on Kickstarter:

> *My Reincarnation* has been a 20-year journey. For two decades I have filmed the esteemed Tibetan Buddhist master, Chögyal Namkhai Norbu, and his son, Khyentse Yeshe, around the world, from Italy to Venezuela, from Russia to Tibet and back again. This film is a never-before seen insider's look at the passing of spiritual knowledge from a Tibetan Master to his Western-born son. It is a positive story of cultural transplantation, adaptation and renewal that gives hope for the future of Tibetan culture in exile.

Again, the question becomes how someone like Jennifer wants to try and raise $50,000 and ends up raising triple that amount with subject matter that may not necessarily appeal to the general audience. One answer is that Jennifer kept up the "twenty years" aspect, which shows potential backers that this project is obviously important, interesting, and inspiring to her as a filmmaker and person. Jennifer most likely also tapped into the right community.

"You Gotta Have Friends"

This is one of the truest lines I've ever heard in a James Cagney film: "I've learned that nobody can do much without somebody else," Paddy Ryan explains to Tom Powers and Matt Doyle in *The Public Enemy*. "Remember this boys, you gotta have friends." We all know this, that in just about every industry you can think of, you need to have friends who'll put in a good word for you and get you to the next level. The DIY filmmaking industry is no exception, especially where crowdfunding is concerned.

A brief look at a few successful high-stakes Kickstarter campaigns shows that they have a large amount of backers supporting their film projects. Look at Ryan Koo and *Man-Child*: 2,336 people backed this project. Jocelyn Towne's crowdfunding campaign for *I Am I* soared $11,965 above its $100,000 Kickstarter goal with the help of 902 backers. Because of 466 backers, filmmaker Jordan Downey will be able to make a sequel to his campy horror comedy *ThanksKilling* about a killer turkey on the prowl that "kills college dorks pun-by-pun." And although there were only 518 backers for *My Reincarnation*, a couple of those were big-money backers at $10,000 a piece, and a solid number of backers contributed between $1,500 and $7,500. It's good to have those kinds of friends when you can find them.

Of course, you get those kinds of friends when you as a filmmaker have some past accomplishments to back you up, as do Jennifer, Jordan, and Koo. Jennifer is an internationally acclaimed producer, director, and camerawoman whose prior documentaries have screened at festivals and have won awards, some of which are listed in more detail on her Kickstarter page for *My Reincarnation*. Jordan has a friend in Gravitas Ventures, which has guaranteed him a distribution deal for the sequel because of the original *ThanksKilling*'s success. And, as Koo mentions in his pitch video as well as in his description of *Man-Child*, he has the support of two internationally known entities: IFP, which named his script one of twenty chosen out of 300 to receive mentorship and access to producers; and The Film Society of Lincoln Center, which selected Koo to be one of twenty-five film-makers to participate in its Emerging Visions program.

That said, if you've got friends like these and your goal is to raise a substantial amount of money for your film project, you shouldn't be too shy about mentioning such acclamations in your pitch video and/or on your campaign's home page.

YOU GOTTA HAVE PATIENCE

As any crowdfunder will tell you, much of the experience of crowdfunding is trial and error. There is really no one right way to crowdfund, though there are a few not-so-right ways, and when things don't go according to plan, patience should be exercised. I brought up things like "The Lull" earlier, those times when it's difficult to push on, which happens to just about every campaign, whether the end goal is $3,000 or $15,000. But at the $100,000 level, patience truly becomes more than a virtue; it becomes a necessity if your campaign is to survive.

Even if you're not using a crowdfunding platform and are going about fundraising on your own website, once you start your campaign, it will no doubt take a little bit of time to build up momentum. Again, a great example is A. D. Lane's *Invasion of the Not Quite Dead*. Through a handful of tweetathons, he's managed to raise a staggering amount of money, and when I was Tweeting with him one day, he confessed that "the Twitter community have been BEYOND amazing, although after thirty months, it's taken PATIENCE."

Sun Tzu states in Chapter Two of *The Art of War* that "if victory is long in coming, then men's weapons will grow dull and their ardor will be damped." Most campaigns should be fought swiftly and diligently, and patience will come into play as three months of crowd-funding winds to an end. But there are exceptions like the *Invasion of the Not Quite Dead* campaign. It's difficult even for me to see so

171

many Tweets about this film project, but if there's one thing Lane's got aside from patience, it's perseverance. The bulk of us are happy to call it quits after three months of crowdfunding, especially if our campaigns get caught in "The Lull" and find no way out. But Lane's weapons surely haven't dulled, and his ardor for his project has not dampened. An anomaly for sure, but one we can all learn something from.

YOU GOTTA HAVE FUN

Yes, crowdfunding is a full-time job. Yes, you won't sleep much. Yes, you may become slightly malnourished. And yes, you may do all of this and not reach your goal. Multiply this exponentially by the size of your end goal, and you might want to turn away from crowd-funding altogether, get a second or third job, and raise the money that way. Despite all of this, crowdfunding can be enjoyable, and most of the time that fun starts with your pitch video and follows through all the way to your perks, promotion, and beyond.

It's no secret that most people like to laugh, especially when watching movies and videos, so when you're putting together your pitch video, try and make them laugh, or at the very least cause them to crack a smile. It doesn't matter if your film is a stoner comedy or as serious in subject matter as Jocelyn Towne's *I Am I*. This movie tells the story of a young woman whose estranged father's mental illness convinces him that she's not his daughter, but his deceased wife. When the girl decides to play along, she begins "to discover the truth about her parents' past and these revelations shed a new light on the present."

The pitch video for *I Am I*, however, is very light and talks nothing about the film itself, but rather how Jocelyn went about getting from script to look book to crowdfunding. From producers popping up from behind her couch and her interrupting her actor-husband in the bathtub to ask if he'd play the lead role to inviting friends and random strangers into their bed as a metaphor for how awkward crowdfunding is ("like asking someone to go to bed with you"), I couldn't help but laugh out loud more than once. At the same time, I also got a sense of how important this story is for Jocelyn, and I saw her passion through the duration of her pitch video. Most importantly, I saw lots of people having fun, and who wouldn't give money to something fun?

Crowdfunding is serious business, yes, but it doesn't have to feel so serious. It's okay to have a good time with your team and your contributors.

You Gotta Have a Story

You may love the story that you want to tell in the film you're crowdfunding for, but to think that everyone will want to hear that story is somewhat unrealistic. We live in a society of niche films, which is a plus since nowadays any and every film that is made will have an audience. But with crowdfunding, you may not want to simply rely on a niche audience. The ultimate question is how do you get someone who doesn't care about sports movies or films that are spiritual in nature to care about and support your film? Easy. You give them another story to be inspired by: *your* story.

This doesn't necessarily mean you should tell people all the intricate details of how you discovered your love of film shooting videos with your high school buddies, which is a bit cliché nowadays. You should tell the story that revolves around the film you want to raise considerable funds for. By doing so, you also address the urgency of the situation and make people ask themselves, "Why should I contribute to this film campaign *now*?"

A prime example of this is Steve Taylor's film adaptation of author Donald Miller's bestselling book *Blue Like Jazz*, a story about "non-religious thoughts on Christian spirituality." The campaign was set up by two fans, Zach Prichard and Jonathan Frazier, with the goal of raising $125,000, the amount needed to make this film.

Originally, *Blue Like Jazz* had two investors at $250,000 each. Then one of them dropped out at the start of preproduction. Not getting too into the "sob" element of this story, Zach and Jonathan's pitch video simply states that "Don announced on his blog that despite a strong screenplay, a stellar cast, and rave reviews, the film would be on hold indefinitely, simply because there was not enough funding."

Then, a giant question mark appears on screen, and with disapproval scratching his voice, Zach poses the ludicrous truth in question, that "they aren't going to make this film because of funding?!" Because of this impressive campaign, Zach and Jonathan brought in a whopping $345,992 with the help of almost 4,500 backers on Kickstarter. What was their focus? Simply put, the absurdity of a film, with a story they and many others believed was worth telling, not being made simply because of a lack of funding. That alone became the anchor that grounded *Blue Like Jazz* in the hearts of over 4,000 backers and helped this massively successful campaign toward amazing new heights and record dollar amounts.

YOU GOTTA HAVE GUTS

Crowdfunding for films like *Blue Like Jazz*, *I Am I*, and *My Reincarnation* takes lots of time, some strategy, and plenty of patience and perseverance, but it also requires the courage to shout to the world, "I need $100,000 to make my film, and I believe that you will give it to me." The minute you think of the other side of the crowdfunding coin — that you might not raise that money — it's over before it's even begun. And with crowdfunding, you not only fail, but you fail in plain sight of everyone you know — your family, your friends, and your social networks.

It was because of doubt and fear that I almost didn't launch my campaign for *Cerise*, and that was for only $5,000. On the $30,000 scale, when the fear factor rises, your self-confidence will freeze up, but we simply can't allow this type of internal paralysis to set in.

A good way to avoid it is to keep in mind that crowdfunding is not about us crowdfunders, but rather the movies we're trying to fund, movies that will be seen by hundreds, perhaps thousands of people worldwide once they're finished; movies that could change lives, make people think differently about certain issues and topics, cause them to see the world, or at the very least their respective worlds, in a different light. If we allow our egos to override this crowdfunding truth, then our movies benefit no one.

Perhaps Jennifer Fox worded it best in an interview she had with Indiewire:

> "Announcing to all the world on the Internet that my film had a deficit was the most naked thing I have ever done," Fox said in a statement. "In the past, I always approached fundraising as a private hush-hush event. Going public really shook up my egotistical concepts of who I was as a person. I started to reflect on that in my blog posts in a way that related to the film's spiritual content."

It doesn't take guts to fail, but it takes guts to succeed. Backers may be drawn to contribute to your campaign by the sheer force of your personality or past accomplishments. Your drive in crowdfunding for your film, however, should not be about you but about the message you're trying to get out into the world — your ideas married to your contributors' support. And yes, it takes guts to send out that first email, Tweet, or Facebook update, and that courage has to stay strong and steady from launch to $30,000 success.

Chapter Thirty-Three

• • •

INDIEGOGO VS. KICKSTARTER

THERE'S A BIT OF A SILENT WAR being waged on the crowd-funding battlefront, and while there are hundreds of platforms out there, there are really only two commanders in the field. That said, perhaps the most pressing of all questions weighing on your brain is which of the two premiere platforms — Indiegogo or Kickstarter — should you go with for your film campaign? For some, there's no question. Others may choose one of the many other platforms like RocketHub, Crowdfunder, or Ulule. Since I've already mentioned in detail the similarities and differences between Indiegogo and Kickstarter in Chapter Eight, I'll jump to the real question on every crowdfunder's mind: *Which platform is better?*

This is an unfair question since, objectively speaking, one platform is not better than another, although I will admit I am partial to Indiegogo in just about every way, from their praiseworthy Customer Happiness Team to their more appealing incentives for reaching one's goal by the specified deadline. But here's the real skinny: for fiction and nonfiction books, graphic novels, causes like Music Against Myeloma, and film projects trying to raise between $5,000 and $25,000, there is no doubt that Indiegogo is the crowdfunding platform I would choose nine times out of ten.

But let's take a look at the one time out of ten when I might consider setting up my crowdfunding camp on Kickstarter's terrain. If my ultimate goal were to raise $30,000 or more for a feature-length film, I would probably choose the crowdfunding platform that has the stronger track record, on which there are more $30,000+ film campaign successes. A Google search will afford you this vital information, as it did for me. That's how I discovered many of the

Kickstarter projects I've mentioned in previous chapters, such as *Blue Like Jazz*, *My Reincarnation*, *ThanksKilling: The Beaquel*, and *I Am I*. There are many others that I didn't bring up, like Nick Broomfield's campaign for his documentary *Sarah Palin: You Betcha!*, which raised $31,120 of a $30,000 goal, and Ricardo and Katie Villarreal's inspiring documentary *Riding with Larry*, which, interestingly enough, brought in $62,695 of a $50,000 Kickstarter goal *and* an additional $10,350 of a $10,000 goal in a separate campaign on Indiegogo.

A Google search for film projects on Indiegogo that have raised $30,000 or more yields only a handful of projects, the most impressive of which is the campaign for *Angry Video Game Nerd: The Movie*, which brought in a staggering $325,927 on a $75,000 goal, the highest-earning film campaign on Indiegogo so far. After an advanced search on Indiegogo's website, I found other projects that have raised some substantial amounts. *Zero Charisma* come out on top with $25,150 raised of their $15,000 target; *Anyone Can Play Guitar* rocked out of its $30,000 campaign with $2,569 in additional funding; *The Joker Blogs*, a popular web series started by Scott McClure and Andrew DeVary, got the last laugh by raising $34,460 of a $25,000 goal; *Walking with Alfred Hassler, Thich Nhat Hanh and Sister Chan Khong* raised $50,065 on their $50,000 goal; and *Bully*, Lee Hirsch's documentary about bullying in America, which received national distribution and recognition at some major festivals, earned $25,580 on a $25,000 goal.

The majority of film projects on Indiegogo, however, tend to raise between $5,000 and $10,000. Two projects of note include Elliot London's *The Wedding Dance*, earning $925 over its $9,000 goal, and a thesis film for Chapman University students called *East of Kensington*, a darker take on the Peter Pan mythos, which brought in $10,492 of its initial goal of $10,000.

Based solely on this information, it seems that for $30,000+ film projects, your best bet probably lies with Kickstarter over Indiegogo. There are a few reasons for why Kickstarter is able to generate this kind of attention. First, it's in the name. Kickstarter plays off of the idea of "kick-starting" your film project, which is very catchy. Second, Kickstarter narrows its focus strictly to creative projects, whereas Indiegogo is much more democratic and allows anyone to crowdfund everything from movies to causes to religions. And while Indiegogo's democratization of fundraising is noble, perhaps Kickstarter's emphasis on film, music, and various other art forms is more appealing to most filmmakers, musicians, and artists, making them feel a stronger connection to a community of artists that may become contributors, supporters, and/or audience members.

Speaking of community, Kickstarter has also jumped one step up on the evolutionary ladder of fundraising by combining crowdfunding with social networking. Crowdfunders and backers of projects can follow other crowdfunders and backers and see which projects they are contributing to. Knowing that your friend just supported Lauren Mora's web series *Misdirected* might make you more likely to check out the Kickstarter campaign for yourself and perhaps put some of your own money into the project. If ten of your friends are supporting that same project, how can you not at least check it out? This sort of thing happens all the time. Through Facebook and Twitter, Gavin Ap'Morrygan has contributed to numerous campaigns on both Indiegogo and Kickstarter because I was supporting those campaigns either financially or socially. This truly is ingenious, and will no doubt keep Kickstarter ahead in the war for crowdfunding glory.

There's also the urgency and curious appeal of Kickstarter's "All or Nothing" deadline, which I mentioned in detail in Chapter Eight. Since there's more at stake if you don't reach your goal and you get nothing for your efforts, many potential contributors may drop the "potential" part and be more willing to become backers of your campaign, not necessarily because they want to see you succeed, but because they don't want to see anyone lose thousands of dollars to an "All or Nothing" deadline. It's all about tension, and we filmmakers know that's what makes a film like *Speed* work so well. By the time we reach the second plot-point of this "hold-your-breath" thrill ride of crowdfunding and we get accustomed to all these "I just backed *Bloodsworth* on Kickstarter" Tweets and updates, we get a little worried as to whether our protagonist (the crowdfunder) will make it. And if we can intervene in any way, chances are, we will.

Of course, Indiegogo also gives crowdfunders the option of choosing an "All or More" deadline, now known as "Flexible Funding," or an "All or Nothing" deadline, known as "Fixed Funding." Clearly, the platform hopes to lure those who prefer Indiegogo's tools and policies but favor the life-and-death nature of Kickstarter's "All or Nothing" deadline to its side of the battlefield. A glance at the majority of campaigns on Indiegogo shows, however, that most people still go with the "Flexible Funding" over "Fixed Funding." After all, that's what Indiegogo's best known for throughout the fundraising community.

From a strictly statistical standpoint, I recommend Kickstarter over Indiegogo if you're looking to raise larger amounts of money for your film project. But no matter what platform you choose, many other factors need to be implemented and executed in order to get your campaign from zero to multiple zeros, and in that sense, my biggest advice would be to do some extra research into these two crowdfunding dynamos. If you're planning on crowdfunding for a feature-length sci-fi film, find out how many projects of that same genre have been funded on each platform. For instance, in my research, I noticed that the majority of projects that get funded on Kickstarter with larger goals are documentaries, not narrative features. On the other hand, a lot more short films seem to find funding on Indiegogo over Kickstarter. This information will change in the coming years, and by the same token, both Indiegogo and Kickstarter will evolve to cater to the needs of their customers. Keep updated on these changes so you can choose the crowdfunding platform that will best suit your film project's needs.

Knowledge is power, after all.

Chapter Thirty-Four

• • •

FISCAL SPONSORSHIP AND THE JOBS ACT: ADDED INCENTIVES FOR CONTRIBUTORS

SOMETIMES A HIGHLY PERSONALIZED PITCH isn't enough to coax a person to click the "Contribute Now" button. Sometimes perks as unique and interesting as the film project itself fall shy of making someone reach for his or her Visa or Master-Card. Sometimes, even tons of fun, quirky promotional Tweets and updates and a well-thought-out marketing strategy just won't make someone become a contributor to your project at anything more than the $10 or $25 level. And at those times, you may need to offer more than what you're currently offering.

FISCAL SPONSORSHIP

Fiscal sponsorship can give potential contributors the ability to contribute to your campaign and write it off as a donation on their tax forms. By partnering up with a non-profit organization like Fractured Atlas, crowdfunders can offer their contributors the added incentive of a charitable deduction for income tax purposes, a service that, individually, they would not be able to offer. Currently, Indiegogo and RocketHub are the two platforms that have partnerships with Fractured Atlas and have been helping filmmakers reach their crowdfunding goals since 2010.

So what exactly are Fractured Atlas and other organizations like it? Rather than try and explain this in the simplest terms possible, I'll let Fractured Atlas give it to you "In a Nutshell" here:

> Fiscal Sponsorship is a financial and legal system by which a legally recognized 501(c)(3) public charity (such as Fractured Atlas) provides limited financial and legal oversight for a project initiated independently by an artist. That "project" might be a one-time project or an independent artist or even an arts organization that does not have its own 501(c)(3) status. Once sponsored in this way, the project is eligible to solicit and receive grants and tax-deductible contributions that are normally available only to 501(c)(3) organizations.

This description of what fiscal sponsorship is and how it works can be found on Fractured Atlas's website, along with much more detailed information, and, more specifically, how its partnerships with Indiegogo and RocketHub work with regard to crowdfunding. But what are the incentives for choosing fiscal sponsorship as opposed to using your crowdfunding platform alone? Aside from the added incentive of a tax deduction, you, the crowdfunder, also get some perks. On Indiegogo, there's a fee of 9% on your total amount raised for using their platform if you don't make your goal; if you do reach your goal, that percentage drops to 4%. By being fiscally sponsored by Fractured Atlas, however, you only pay 6% to Fractured Atlas, and Fractured Atlas covers all of Indiegogo's fees for you. So in the end, by being sponsored by Fractured Atlas, if you happen to not reach your crowdfunding goal, you'll end up paying 3% less than you would had you run your campaign without being sponsored by this 501(c)(3) organization.

Another incentive for you as a crowdfunder is that Fractured Atlas also gives you access to foundation and government grants that may only be accessible to non-profit organizations or fiscally sponsored projects. This means that you can raise some money through crowdfunding, which will also give you an early opportunity to build a following and a fan base for when your film is finished. You can also take the more traditional route and try to obtain grants and scholarships, which may ultimately give you even more money to work with on your film project in the long run, and if you run a successful crowdfunding campaign, of course.

There is much more detailed information available on Fractured Atlas's website (*www.fracturedatlas.org*), so you can read up on the inner workings of fiscal sponsorship and decide whether it would be a good option for your film project.

THE JOBS ACT

Then there's the JOBS (Jumpstart Our Business Startups) Act, signed into law by President Barack Obama in 2012. This legislation makes it possible for investors to invest equity into small businesses via the Internet in an attempt to jumpstart the American economy and create new jobs and a more financially stable country. What does this mean for crowdfunders of short and feature-length films? You will now be able to offer a return on investment to anyone who comes on board as an equity investor. Instead of offering those funders the T-shirt or DVD perks in exchange for their $50 or $100 contribution, you can offer something more appealing to an investor: a share in your film's profits.

Currently, the JOBS Act is strictly being developed for business startups, but because the law revolves specifically around the concept of crowdfunding, it will ultimately affect every aspect of online fundraising, from small startups to short films. Industry experts, business lawyers, and crowd leaders regularly post content about the JOBS Act, especially since the Securities and Exchange Commission (SEC) and the Crowdfunding Accreditation for Platform Standards (CAPS), two major participants in the establishment of crowdfunding bylaws, are currently firming up procedures for properly governing online fundraising. That said, I highly recommend keeping a close eye on the frequently changing landscape of crowdfunding. Two trustworthy sites you should subscribe to are *www.crowdsourcing.org* and The Daily Crowdsource (*www.dailycrowdsource.com*), and/or follow them on Twitter (@Crowdsourcing_ and @TDCrowdsource, respectively), which will help keep you in the know on all things related to crowdfunding.

Chapter Thirty-Five

...

ENHANCING YOUR TEAM

IN CHAPTER SIX I discussed the idea of forming a central team of people who support you and your film project 100%. Much like there's no "I" in "Team," there's no chapter in *The Art of War* that talks about a one-man army corps. In war, you need an army of soldiers the way in filmmaking you need a crew. In crowdfunding, as well, it helps to have a core of people who will split the numerous duties involved with launching and sustaining a successful crowdfunding campaign.

If you're aiming to raise some substantial bucks for your film project, you may want to enhance your team in a variety of ways. Or rather teams, since it might be a good idea to have as many as three teams as part of your campaign: your A-Team, in which you are Colonel "Hannibal" Smith leading a small band of skilled soldiers onto the frontlines; your B-Team, comprised of foot soldiers who can keep the work going through the hours and minutes of your campaign; and your C-Team ("C" for "crowd," of course), made up of allies from your crowd, most likely people who have gone from potential to full-blown contributors.

THE A-TEAM

Your A-Team should consist of the main people who are going to be pushing your campaign the most, giving their 110% to every Tweet, status update, and email blast they drive out into the social stream. If phone calls need to be made, they'll be the ones making them. Meg Pinsonneault's A-Team of producer/publicist Lindsey Rowe and cinematographer Sabina Padilla promoted *Gwapa* (*Beautiful*) nonstop from the beginning of the project's crowdfunding campaign. They didn't simply push hard during its final days and hours. From day one they were on the frontlines for a project they unwaveringly believed in.

East of Kensington's A-Team consists of seven solid members, including a person in charge of their social media promotions:

The A-Team crowing behind East of Kensington *on Indiegogo.*

Again, my A-Team for *Cerise* was made up of myself, Marinell, the campaign's primary marketing person, and Alain, the film's cinematographer. Alain not only helped spread the word through Tweets and Facebook updates, but also wrote a couple of blog posts detailing what he and I were hoping to accomplish visually with *Cerise*, including some posts consisting of photos of our location scouts to get his network of camera-savvy cinematographers and photographers more excited about his next project.

The B-Team

It's no secret that some aspects of crowdfunding are time-consuming and not very interesting. Or sometimes you're crowdfunding while at the same time trying to contact sponsors, individuals, and other institutions to get them to donate something you would like to offer as a special-incentive perk. Other times you may be trying to apply for grants, and filling out that paperwork can take time away from the more pressing matter of spreading the word about your film campaign.

Enter your B-Team, which I might suggest filling up with volunteers or unpaid interns. They can take care of some of the additional tasks involved with securing funding for your film. Volunteers are preferred because, in theory, they actually want to be a part of your project, and no matter how mundane you may think the duties you're assigning to them are, they will most likely be thankful to play any role whatsoever in the process of filmmaking. Plus, they'll be learning a lot about alternative methods of fundraising which they themselves might make use of for their own films.

Interns are like volunteers in that they might take part in your film project for the knowledge they will walk away with in exchange for their services during your campaign. You may want them to actively help with the crowdfunding, or you may want them to be the ones filling out the paperwork for various film and artist grants. This way, they'll learn how to fill out that paperwork and also grow accustomed to sending professional emails to organizations, which they may make use of in the future for their film projects. Furthermore, by doing this, they will leave your campaign with a network of contacts in the process. Learning how to chat about your film project with potential backers might even give them the confidence they need to pitch their own ideas over the phone at a later date.

You may think finding an intern is difficult. As someone who has used interns in the past, I find it's a fairly simple process and you don't have to work at a university to be able to hire one. You simply have to go to the cooperative education representative at any college or university in your area and fill out some paperwork, which students will then peruse, and, based on the information you supply, will choose whether they'd like to intern for you. You don't have to pay the interns, since they will be given college credit for the professional work experience, but you may want to treat them to lunch and offer a weekly stipend for their commute. It's that easy, and will make the process of crowdfunding that $30,000 and simultaneously applying for grants a little less stressful.

THE C-TEAM

The C-Team, or Crowd-Team, is pulled together during your crowdfunding campaign and is comprised of people who have become contributors or those who are strong supporters of your project. Many of these people may even be able to offer more than a contribution or series of retweets, both during and long after your campaign. For instance, Ben Gerber's most recent gift to *Cerise* was the URL "*http://watch.CeriseMovie.com*" so we could more easily get people to see my short film. Had I been trying to raise upward of $30,000, I would've sent Ben a message asking him if I could list him as a team member on our Indiegogo page as well, much the way we eventually listed our composer Nino Rajacic, who donated the score to the film.

The C-Team is anything but C-grade, and depending on how well you get to know the people you may be thinking of recruiting for your campaign, you may discover that they are very talented as well as humble and supportive. I always refer back to Charles Simon's project *Deader Days*, which I mentioned in Chapter Six, and how he asked me in a direct message on Twitter if he could add me to his team as "Doctor of Prosaic Rhythm." Don't be afraid to recruit the people you see going to bat for you and your campaign. The larger the army, the larger the outreach, and the closer you'll be to conquering your crowdfunding goal.

CELEBRITY TEAMMATES

For projects trying to raise a significant amount of money, usually about $50,000 to $100,000 or more, it doesn't hurt to bring a few celebrities into your campaign. I'm not necessarily talking about getting an indie star like @edward_burns to come on board your team and Tweet out a few links to your film campaign — obviously that wouldn't happen. But "celebrity" is an interesting notion nowadays. There's really no such thing as a famous person *everyone* knows. But in the indie film community, there are plenty of filmmakers who've done wonderful things, who've won awards, and who would no doubt help a filmmaker with his or her crowdfunding efforts. If it's possible, those are the kinds of celebrities you may want to get hooked up with your project.

Keep in mind, however, that just because you have a "real" celebrity — like a well-known movie and television personality — it doesn't guarantee an easy way out of crowdfunding for your film project. The Indiegogo campaign for $12,000 in finishing funds for Sam Graydon's short film *Jenny*, starring film legend Gary Busey, brought in only 10% of its goal. And even *30 Rock* star Kevin Brown couldn't get the Indiegogo campaign for a pilot episode of superhero spoof *Capes and Claims* soaring any further past $460 of the $7,700 its campaigners hoped to raise, perhaps through Brown's notoriety alone. Successful crowdfunding, basic or advanced, will always take a team effort.

When you're raising significant amounts of money through crowdfunding, you have to have a diehard team. The more teammates you can muster up, the more potential contributors you will have to win over, because every team member you bring into your campaign has his or her own network. If you've got team members who have won film awards or those who are fortunate enough to have worked with slightly more famous names in the film industry, it boosts your chances of success, but does not guarantee it. Exploit these facts the right way by mentioning them in your Indiegogo or Kickstarter campaign, but not harping on them, and you will most likely draw in more views for a look at your pitch and a lift in your funds.

Chapter Thirty-Six

· · ·

BRINGING YOUR
CAMPAIGN OFFLINE

LIKE MY FRIEND who ran one of the unsuccessful crowd-funding campaigns mentioned in the blog post he wrote for Film Courage, sometimes "Twitter & Facebook alone will NOT get your film funded on Kickstarter or Indiegogo." That said, whether you're trying to raise $10,000, like he was, or $50,000 for your ambitious feature-length movie, sometimes you may not be able to rely solely on the Internet. You may have to go back to the old grassroots methods and bring your campaign offline as well. I don't mean you should opt out of your campaign during the first hour of "The Lull." I mean that while you are crowdfunding on-line, it might not hurt to vary your fundraising techniques and do some traditional fundraising "in the real world."

Below are three simple ways you can bring your campaign offline while continuing to build up awareness of your online crowd-funding efforts.

CAMPAIGN CARDS, POSTCARDS, AND OTHER PRINT MATERIAL

In 2011, I attended New York Comic Con and I ran into my friend and *Cerise* superhero Gavin Ap'Morrygan. While we were waiting on line to get our copies of *The Walking Dead* signed by Robert Kirkman, I asked him what he's been up to. He reached into his wallet and pulled out a business card for a film he was helping to crowdfund called *Ninjas vs Monsters*, which I'd mentioned in an earlier chapter.

I was impressed that Gavin was officially on the team for this third and final installment of this *Ninjas vs* trilogy. I flipped the card over from the side that brandished the official *Ninjas vs Monsters* logo and their customized URL *www.NinjasWin.com*, which brings you to the Kickstarter page, and saw Gavin's name, phone number, and email address, as well as his "Producer" title.

All the pertinent information to help fund Ninjas vs Monsters *is on the back of Gavin's card.*

Having a business card on you at all times while you're running your crowdfunding campaign is important because you never know who you're going to run into, or when or where, for that matter. If you get into a conversation with a random person at a cocktail party and tell him or her about your film project and campaign and that person seems interested in contributing, it won't benefit anyone for you to say "go to Ninjas Win dot com." After a few drinks and a ton of handshakes, there's little certainty this person will even remember you, let alone your project information. On the other hand, if you've got your campaign card ready to hand out with your URL on both sides, as Gavin did, and a catchy phrase in the vein of "YOU can be a part of this AMAZING film!", then you've got the upper hand and possibly another contributor in a few hours or the following day.

While I was in Los Angeles for a screening of *Cerise* alongside the crowdfunded feature-length film *Tilt*, I spoke with my friend Gregor Collins about his crowdfunding campaign for a film called *It's a Good Day to Die*. He, as well, reached into his wallet and pulled out a campaign card — a very cool campaign card, too.

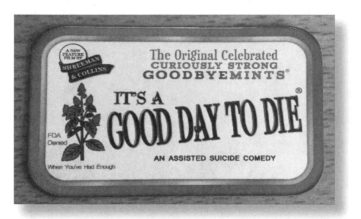

A little design goes a long way, as evidenced by Gregor Collins' card for It's a Good Day to Die.

At first glance, the card looks like an Altoids tin, and the card itself even has the beveled edges of one of those collectible containers. But a closer examination unveils that instead of "Altoids" there's the title of the film; where it would normally read "The Original Celebrated Curiously Strong Peppermints," here the word "pepper" is replaced with "goodbye"; and where an Altoids tin is produced by "Callard & Bowser," Gregor's goodbye mints are made by "Shreeman & Collins." Brilliant design, all in a campaign card that evokes a company noted for its offbeat advertising campaigns.

The reverse side of this card features instructions on what to search for on Google for people who'll be checking it out on their computers at home. It also displays a QR code that can be captured by a smartphone using a QR code-scanning app like RedLaser. So if Gregor gives his card to someone with a smart phone, he or she can scan it right then and there and make a contribution to his film campaign, all in a matter of minutes. That's what I call efficiency!

Type these words into Google:
"Good Day to Die Kickstarter"
to watch our Kickstarter video.

Or just capture the QR code. ---->

Campaign Begins: 9-26-11
Campaign Ends: 11-11-11

We know you're *dying* to come aboard...

As with Gavin's card, all the necessary information is on the back of Gregor's card, plus a QR code for more immediate access to his campaign.

I never really needed to bring my crowdfunding campaign for *Cerise* offline and into the real world, though I know that if I had, I could've gotten even more funding and would have reached my goal a lot sooner. A colleague of mine at one of the universities where I teach always told me whenever we'd stop and chat briefly in between classes, "Put me down for fifty bucks." I never got his fifty bucks, however, because he's busy and kept forgetting, and he didn't really know what crowdfunding was or how to contribute. Had I given him a campaign card like Gavin's or Gregor's, he might have remembered to take five minutes and make the contribution. In this case, having a physical reminder would've been a huge benefit.

"SURPRISE" PHONE CALLS

The personal touch doesn't get more personal than with a phone call. If you're campaigning online, posting update upon update, Tweet upon (re)tweet, and making them sing a different song each time, and if you're sending email updates every few days but still not making much headway toward your goal, then it's time to switch off the Internet for an hour or so and make a couple of phone calls.

Obviously, this phone call will not be just to say, "Hi, how have you been?" and play the catch-up game. You have something at stake: thousands of dollars that need to be raised from kindhearted people like the one you're about to call. So this phone call has to be natural at the beginning, and at one point smoothly transition into a very personable pitch. A phone call like this is similar to "Friend Fawning" on Facebook, which we learned about in Chapter Twenty-Eight. The only difference is that your confidence, passion, and drive for your film project must come across in voice rather than writing or images, and for some, especially in a world driven by words typed as text messages, Tweets, and emails, this can sometimes be more difficult than ever.

Nonetheless, it will be that personal outreach that will show your potential contributors who you are as a person before you show them who you want to be as a filmmaker, and being a crowdfunder is the bridge between the two. One thing to note is that this call probably won't last ten minutes. Remember, this isn't telemarketing, and nobody likes those people anyway, so you want to avoid the fine line between communicating and marketing. After you catch up for a few minutes, you'll want to spend the next minute or two communicating (or pitching) your film instead of trying to market your film like a product.

That's the personal touch that should get just about anyone to at least listen to what you have to say. Sometimes just hearing the sincerity in someone's voice as he or she describes a project passionately is a refreshing change from the direction in which our society is headed. A "LOL" appended at the end of a text message is always a good thing, but it doesn't come close to the sound of someone actually laughing out loud because of something you said. It's this kind of interaction that can mean the difference between a $10 contribution and receiving the final $100 you need for a successful campaign.

THE HANDSHAKE

If you're raising money but your home base is somewhere in Austin, Texas, chances are you'll have little choice but to rely on your social network and email contacts. The other option is to spend some money on travel and lodging and get yourself to where some of the potential high-rolling contributors and investors spend their days and nights. Even if you're located in New York City like me, you still may need to journey west to Los Angeles if you've been meeting or Tweeting some contacts online who don't seem to be supportive in terms of contributions.

I'm not advising that you book a flight to LA to see some guy you've spoken to only a handful of times who happens to be a mirror image of yourself. You're going for the big bucks at $30,000 and over, so you should seek out entrepreneur-types who may have some money to contribute to your film campaign. You, in turn, can help further their names in the world of indie film by adding another notch to their film production belt, and if they're living and working in LA or New York, it's a pretty safe bet that they want to do this as a career. If you've met many people like these who are situated in one place and who've expressed interest in your film project and/or your crowdfunding campaign tactics, I suggest you be prepared to call and set up some meetings with them, all within a long weekend or full week, and swipe a credit card for a plane ticket, hotel, car (you'll need one in LA), and a nice blouse or blazer.

A phone call imbues your campaign with your voice. A handshake impresses your personal seal onto another person. Again, the personal touch is something that tends to get lost in the digital age. If you're willing to go the extra few thousand miles from Texas to California or from Seattle to New York City, loaded with campaign cards and a pitch that sounds more like a conversation, producers and other potential contributors will pick up on this, and you just might be surprised by the results.

The other option for reaching out your hands to meet and greet potential contributors to your film project is to attend a film festival. I don't mean attending your town's first-year film festival, because chances are it'll be filled with more filmmakers than film producers who have the kind of money and clout you're hoping to secure for your current project. I'm talking about the tried and tested ones like Sundance, Tribeca, and SXSW. Yes, it will cost quite a bit of money, but again, and to quote Charles Kemper's character in Nicholas Ray's *On Dangerous Ground*, "If you want something out of this life you gotta put something in it from the heart."

Attend Sundance Film Festival, go to the seminars, and rub elbows with anyone you can meet. Get their business cards, follow them on Twitter, and then see how much new support you've got for your crowdfunding campaign. In Wisconsin, for instance, there's a wonderful festival called Flyway Film Festival, and every year many people from New York City, Los Angeles, and other big cities in between flock there to watch cutting-edge films, attend informative seminars, and meet and greet one another. You never know whose hand you might end up shaking — that person could be someone who contributes a substantial amount to your current or future campaign, or even someone you may end up working with on a bigger project. When you weigh what you put into a trip like that with what you might get out of it, it all balances out.

With crowdfunding as with filmmaking, everything should be in balance. You should use your platform and all the online tools at your disposal, but mix in a personal phone call to break the impersonal wall of typewritten words. Get used to this, and perhaps you'll be giving your campaign card to a newfound contributor you met at Sundance who may be able to help make your project superior to all others.

Chapter Thirty-Seven

...

CONSECUTIVE CAMPAIGNING, TRANSMEDIA, AND BEYOND

FOR MORE AMBITIOUS FILM PROJECTS, you will most likely have to change up your tactics a bit more and think ahead into the future of crowdfunding, filmmaking, and storytelling. Maybe you want to raise money for a couple of your next short or feature-length film projects back to back to keep up your appearance as a working filmmaker. Maybe you want to explore the possibilities of transmedia, or multi-platform storytelling, as a means to bring in more potential contributors and build an even stronger, more engaged following not only for your film but for every incarnation the story of your film embraces. To be active DIY filmmakers, you have to be active crowdfunders, and here's how to achieve that kind of activity.

CONSECUTIVE CAMPAIGNING

If you're like me, you probably come up with a new logline or ten every day for a film or web series that you feel is a stroke of genius and would make for a lucrative project. Then, after about a week of brushing away all the loglines that couldn't extend their wings and become whole synopses, you may be left with two or three really solid ideas that might be worth pursuing. If you've got the time, the network, a few big spenders, and a strong support system for your prior work, you may be able to run consecutive campaigns like filmmakers Mattson Tomlin and Charles Simons did for their film projects. Mattson started out with a Kickstarter campaign called "Bring *Solomon Grundy* to Life" in January of 2010 and successfully raised $12,064 of his initial $10,000 goal by April.

A mere five months later, he launched his second campaign for another short film called *Dream Lover* and exceeded his Kickstarter goal of $8,422 by six dollars.

Charles Simons launched his Indiegogo campaign for his comedy web series *Duhmfownd* around August of 2011 and brought in $1,600 of the $1,300 he deemed necessary to film two subsequent episodes of the series. Shortly after reaching his crowdfunding goal, Charles launched his campaign for *Deader Days* in September, a mere month after his prior success, and again he was successful, raising $7,537 of a $7,500 goal.

While it appears that consecutive campaigning can lead to success, it doesn't hurt to briefly examine the level of success. In each of the cases above, Mattson and Charles raised substantial amounts over their goals for *Solomon Grundy* and *Duhmfownd*, $2,064 and $300, respectively. However, during their second campaigns, they both reached their goals, but barely made it a few dollars over the hump — *Dream Lover* brought in an additional $6; *Deader Days* $37. What might a third consecutive campaign have yielded?

There may be something to be said about taking a little break after one or at most two campaigns, especially if it's your first time crowdfunding. You want to work your friends, followers, and supporters into the whole idea that you're taking to the Internet to raise funds to make your film, but you don't want to overwork them too soon, either. Crowdfunding is like exercising a muscle. If you push it too hard, you'll be sore the next morning, or worse, you might pull something and possibly do more severe damage. Most people have no qualms about supporting a film project simply to give the filmmaker a chance at the big time. If, however, you want them to contribute again, it may behoove you as a crowdfunder to wait a while until you have some proof that your next film will be a winner like the first film their contributions helped make happen.

Then there's a film project like Gary King's *How Do You Write a Joe Schermann Song*, which raised a grand total of $49,132 between two campaigns. This makes for an impressive exception to the cautions of consecutive campaigning, but there's more about those two campaigns in my crowd study "How Do You Direct [A Gary King Musical] — Build Your Brand."

TRANSMEDIA STORYTELLING

I first learned about transmedia when I attended an event called DIY Days, organized by filmmaker Lance Weiler. One of the seminar speakers, Jeff Gomez of Starlight Runner Entertainment, told a moving story about how, when he was a boy, he was fascinated by a Japanese manga hero called Kikaider. He had read the entire comic book series and realized that the publisher wasn't planning on printing another issue. The problem was that the story wasn't finished. He then learned that the Kikaider series would continue as a television series and would pick up where the last issue had left off. Watching episode after episode of the show that featured his favorite comic-book-hero-turned-TV-star, Jeff was a happy boy until the TV series came to an end. Once again, however, the story itself was far from finished. The TV series, it turned out, was going to be concluded as a feature-length movie.

Transmedia, or multi-/cross-platform storytelling, has been around since long ago, and it has resurfaced stronger than ever in a time when story is king and how you get that story across to your audience relies heavily on the use of new media, modern technology, and advanced storytelling techniques. Like Jeff's favorite superhero going from print to TV to film, today there are plenty of other platforms to consider making use of to convey different parts of the overall story you want to tell. The Internet, mobile devices, video games, and even social networks can all be used to create a larger story experience, which can extend the outreach of your film world and invite audiences that enjoy those different forms of entertainment to follow your story through all its manifold parts.

With regard to crowdfunding, transmedia can be used in a variety of contexts. Most crowdfunders use websites like Vimeo and YouTube to push out update, behind-the-scenes, and other kinds of video to their contributors. These videos are usually password-protected, making the experience seem more exclusive to those who've contributed, but they seldom add anything to the story of the films themselves. By incorporating transmedia into your campaign, you can add new layers to your storyworld that are not necessarily integral to your film but offer further insight into the story, characters, or both.

An interesting example, though regrettably unsuccessful as an Indiegogo campaign, is the transmedia project *Whiz!Bam!Pow!*, based on the idea of an old-school spinner rack. According to writer, producer, and director Tyler Weaver, "instead of being filled with comic books, it's filled with every form of media we can find to tell our story — delivered directly to you, whenever you want to visit the world of *Whiz!Bam!Pow!*" Some of the various types of media *Whiz!Bam!Pow!* would imbue with nostalgia include comic books, of course, but also radio shows, short films, prose, web serials, and even advertising.

Tyler eventually pushed *Whiz!Bam!Pow!* into the world in the summer of 2012 after raising only $3,205 of his $15,000 crowdfunding goal. So far, he's created a comic book, *Whiz!Bam!Pow! Comics #7*, which introduces Tyler's fictional 1938 superhero The Sentinel as the central figure in the storyworld of *Whiz!Bam!Pow!* He's also generated a handful of chapters, written in prose, that tell a more contemporary story rooted in the comics world that will unfold through an assortment of other media.

Perhaps one of the main reasons for Tyler's lack of success with his Indiegogo campaign for *Whiz!Bam!Pow!* is that he really didn't make the campaign as creative and innovative as the project itself. Despite the personalized $75 perk, which makes the funder's name the secret

Transmedia storyteller Tyler Weaver imbues everything related to Whiz!Bam!Pow! *with nostalgia, even the advertisements.*

identity of a member of The Sentinel's super team, the perks do not make much use of transmedia storytelling and instead are simple and standard. For instance, episodes of the radio show are offered as perks, but those would be made available for anyone to hear, whether you're a contributor or not.

The link between crowdfunding and transmedia has not yet been inked and colored in, only sketched out in pencil, but in the near future perhaps crowdfunding will be used as a transmedia platform. Transmedia can already be used in crowdfunding to help build a following for your film by offering potential contributors options for immersing themselves in your project before it's made and, as mentioned earlier, supplying them with background into your film's storyworld. After all, if they become invested in your story through exclusive video content, games, and other forms of media, potential contributors may be more likely to become full-fledged contributors.

More and more, transmedia, like crowdfunding, is becoming highly personalized and interactive, and it's only a matter of time before crowdfunders start architecting "crowdfunding experiences" around their campaigns. Filmmakers already offer exclusive content once their films are available to the public, but not while they're crowdfunding for them. By offering unique perks to engage your audience in the storyworld of your film, you combine the best of crowdfunding with the best of what transmedia can offer. This content can come in various forms, such as a page from a character's diary, which can be much more engaging story-wise than a signed script for a $50 contribution. Another option, if you've already cast your film, is to have your actors, in character, record videos that divulge some inside information about their lives, perhaps giving deeper insight into those characters and thus forming a stronger bond between funder/audience member and character and film. You might even offer a perk in which a character will phone a contributor and tell him or her a secret that will be between them — a secret that may be integral to more thoroughly understanding the story of your film.

One Indiegogo project on the precipice of combining transmedia storytelling with crowdfunding was *Twenty Million People*, a feature-length film by Michael Ferrell, Devin Sanchez, and Chris Pine. The campaign offered a very personalized, interactive perk at the $25 level based around a choose-your-own-adventure-style storybook. *Twenty*

Million People is a romantic comedy centered on the idea that it's difficult to find someone you want to be with amidst a city twenty million strong. This particular perk gives contributors the opportunity to be a character in their very own romantic comedy. Michael writes up a first act in second-person narration and offers you a choice at the end of it. Once you choose how you'd like to proceed, Michael writes a second act based around that choice and gives you one final choice to make that will lead to the ending of your choosing. This is similar to the fundamental concept of transmedia, that when we tell stories to our friends, we tweak those stories ever so slightly based on the reaction of the audience. Here, Michael gives you options and bases your romantic comedy's progression on those choices, which are reactions to what was previously written for you.

I see *Twenty Million People* as a precursor to the endlessly creative ways of using transmedia in crowdfunding because of its $25 perk and also because the perk itself fits in with the overall theme of the film. In fact, over 100 of the campaign's 173 funders chose perks at $25 and up. That's over 100 rom-coms written and over 100 funders who now have a deeper connection to Michael's film and storyworld because they are part of the "twenty million people" who make up the title of the film.

The use of transmedia in crowdfunding has a ways to go before it becomes the norm, but based on current transmedia trends like *geocaching* — using GPS to find physical clues to unlock mysteries of a storyworld — *gamification* — the use of games as a storytelling tool — and *augmented reality* — the blending of the real and digital worlds — people will be searching for new ways to bring not only money into their campaigns, but contributors into their films.

The crowdfunding campaign for my next film project aims to do just that. I'll be raising funds to make three short films in a trilogy about memory. Two of the three films are already written and ready to shoot, but the third is only a vague idea that needs development. While I crowdfund the money to make the two films, I'll be crowdsourcing ideas for the third by offering a perk that allows the contributor to tell me a memory that I will work into my third film, thus directly making my audience part of my trilogy's storyworld.

Much the way crowdfunding is partly about fundraising and partly about audience outreach, transmedia is one part spreading your story across multiple platforms and one part creating a bridge between your film and its audience by immersing them in a larger story. If you can get your funders to invest in a world and not just a film, they will build a world around not only your film's story, but also all the forms your story encompasses, from video games to mobile apps. This will give you a larger crowd from which to draw in more funding and surpass your goal and maybe even your greatest expectations.

· PART SIX ·
SUMMARY POINTS

- To raise $30,000+ on Indiegogo or Kickstarter, you "gotta have" a gimmick, friends, patience, fun, and most importantly, guts.

- Added incentives for contributions such as fiscal sponsorship through a 501(c)(3) non-profit organization like Fractured Atlas can help certain projects raise more substantial amounts and possibly reach their goals faster.

- When crowdfunding for considerable funds, it may be wise to have three teams at your side: your A-Team, or direct team; your B-Team, comprised of volunteers and/or interns; and your C-Team, the crowd-based team.

- Bring your campaign offline into the "real" world with campaign cards and other print materials, surprise phone calls, and, of course, a handshake whenever possible.

• Transmedia storytelling and consecutive campaigning can be used to help build a greater brand and story not only for your film project, but also for its crowdfunding campaign, distribution, and beyond.

· Part Six ·
EXERCISE

Think about your story and campaign. How can you combine the two for a grander transmedia experience? What other forms of media, such as short film/trailer, app, graphic novel, and short story to name a few, might this story adopt to help build a wider audience for and awareness of both your film and its crowdfunding campaign?

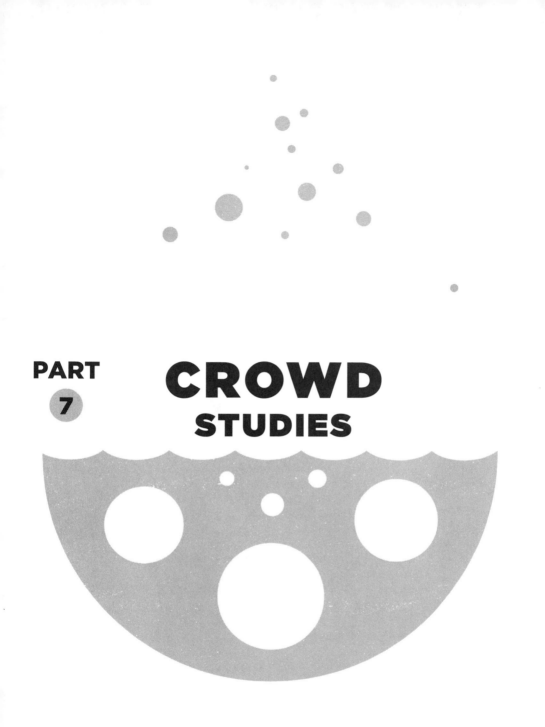

PART 7 CROWD STUDIES

• • •

AT HOME AWAY FROM HOME:
TILT THE TOWN

DURING ITS KICKSTARTER CAMPAIGN, *Tilt* was first billed as "an independent film collaboration" because it brought together a trio of talented DIY filmmakers to create the "independent thriller" *Tilt* would become after raising $15,606. Julie Keck and Jessica King, the writing and filmmaking duo behind their company King is a Fink Productions, teamed up with filmmaker Phil Holbrook after some conversations on Twitter about possibly working together on a project. The only thing that separated Phil from these two architects of mischief was physical distance — Julie and Jessica hail from Chicago while Phil is situated in the small town of Brainerd, Minnesota. But even that didn't stop them. Julie and Jessica took off to Brainerd to talk about what would ultimately be a successful gathering from which *Tilt* the film and crowdfunding campaign would emerge.

But that's not all that materialized. During the scriptwriting process, Jessica had been thinking of ways to play with the *Tilt* story outside of the movie, seeing as how transmedia storytelling is the way to grab hold of an audience these days. She devised *Tilt* the Town, and it was later when they were talking about possible perks for the Kickstarter campaign that *Tilt* the Town came up again. That's when they decided to roll with it, not knowing how successful an incentive it would be to make people contribute to *Tilt* the crowdfunding campaign.

WHAT IS *TILT* THE TOWN?

Tilt *the Town and the folks who "live" there come to life as a Google Map thanks to Julie Keck and Jessica King.*

Tilt the Town is a virtual town created from a map of Phil's hometown of Brainerd. The difference is that this town is populated by characters from the film and mapped by specific landmarks used in the film, such as The Last Turn Saloon and the convenience store where Paul, the main character, buys his groceries. There are also landmarks that are not in the film, like Bump & Grind, a coffee shop/dance studio where retired ballerina Sheri Candler teaches, and Lock-N-Load, Jake Stetler's microbrewery.

And who are Sheri Candler and Jake Stetler? They're just two of 170 Kickstarter backers-turned-*Tilt* the Towners by the writing prowess of King is a Fink. Every backer who contributed $15 to the *Tilt* crowdfunding campaign received a personalized bio about his or her role in *Tilt* the Town. For many crowdfunders, this may have been too much effort to put into one single backer, never mind 170 of them. Even Julie and Jessica admit they had no idea how much work would go into it, or how successful it would ultimately be. But it was this level of personalization that made *Tilt* the Town the successful enterprise is was. There's that, and the fact that Julie and Jessica did so at such a low pledge amount. Most crowdfunders might consider doing something of this magnitude at the $50 or $100 perk level, but not at $15, which just about everyone can afford. Look at the detail of my bio, for instance:

> Backer #21: John Trigonis was the 1st person from his family to graduate from Harvard Law School. Amongst his very brainy friends, he was the very 1st to pass the bar (the 1st time), the 1st to land a fancy job, and the 1st...no, ONLY one to walk out of the courtroom and quit his job after the 1st day of his 1st case.

> It's not that John wasn't good at it; it's that he knew he was going to win. John was defending a large fishing conglomerate from Brainerd aquaculturist Roger Hjulstrom's accusation that their practices were unsafe to local species. John knew that he could counter Roger's claims and even stick him with the Fish Inc.'s legal bill, but it just didn't feel like the right thing to do. So he quit.

> His adoring parents supported his decision, of course (they love their little Johnny), but they were a little taken aback when John announced that he wanted to move to Brainerd to be the resident puppeteer. However, John thought being a career puppeteer was only logical. He could make up stories, make his puppets fight, and then make them make up at the end, without messy legal entanglements. Happily ever after.

> John hosts his puppet shows from an elaborate hand-built stage which he pulls around town on the back of his motorcycle. The stage box is just big enough for him to hide himself in while his puppets tell his stories. The stage box also serves as his home. There he sleeps, usually parked under the Brainerd Water Tower, amongst his puppets. Once in a

while he spends the night at Marinell Montales' new condo, waking her up with breakfast in bed and finger puppet love songs. Sometimes he lunches with Andrew Bichler. Sometimes he just sits and celebrates the day he quit being a lawyer.

Admittedly, this is a fancy bit of story to tell for one backer, but aside from the bios, Julie and Jessica wanted to keep their audience, backers, and followers fully engaged, so they continued writing more stories, involving more and more interactions between backers. For instance, Marinell's my girlfriend and Andrew Bichler's a friend and *Cerise* supporter, but I've never met Roger Hjulstrom; yet, in *Tilt* the Town, I'm interacting with him in some virtual way, which can lead to further interaction outside of *Tilt* the Town, in the real world. This not only builds up King is a Fink and Phil Holbrook's following on Twitter and Facebook, but also connects others to those networks, which in the future could lead to other collaborations like *Tilt*. In most instances, Julie and Jessica end each bio with, "Learn more about the real Eric here" and link us to a website, blog, or other page where we can get to know our fellow *Tilt* backers.

Tilt the Town is really quite ingenious in that sense. By mentioning a new Kickstarter backer on Twitter using his or her handle and by appending #TiltTheTown to your Tweet, you're given a key to an entire town being run by a pair of creative, dedicated, and just plain fun young ladies. Yes, they control the stories that are told; in a perfect world, they would have liked it for others to interact with one another without King is a Fink being an intermediary, but it would've been very messy in terms of organization. But this truly dynamic crowdfunding duo did a stellar job at building up a considerable following of people and attracting the attention of other individuals in the indie film world, some of whom Julie and Jessica have recently collaborated with on other projects.

HOW SUCCESSFUL WAS *TILT* THE TOWN?

Julie shared with me a very interesting fact about *Tilt* the Town: "Many people who originally contributed less than $15 eventually upped their pledges to get in on the fun." That says a lot about the success of *Tilt* the Town, not only because people raised their pledge amounts, but because it wasn't the kind of increase that would break the bank. Even if a person had pledged $10, which grants that person regular updates on *Tilt's* progress and his or her name in the end credits of the film, for only $5 more he or she would unlock a door into a fun-filled virtual reality.

The advent of *Tilt* the Town and all the stories that Julie and Jessica wove into the fabric of their social network created a sort of *Tilt* the Experience that people would not only want in on, but also would want to know more about. For instance, in a description of the actual characters of *Tilt*, we're introduced to a whole bunch of strange and interesting inhabitants of the town. Then we'll notice something called "Crime Scene #1" and then its mysterious description below: "We know you're curious, but please step back behind the caution tape." It's little things like this, situated snugly between in-depth descriptions of The Last Turn Saloon, the police station, and detailed character narratives that pique our interest in the progression of the *Tilt* storyline. That, and the fact that we remember the tagline from the pitch video — "Where do you bury your secrets?" — tell us that something's not right in the state of *Tilt* the Town, yet here we are, in one form or another, waiting in anticipation for something to happen.

TWO YEARS LATER: IS *TILT* THE TOWN A BURIED SECRET?

Tilt the Town is alive and well and living in Brainerd, MN, near Chicago, IL, in Jersey City, NJ, and any- and everywhere there's an Internet connection. Julie and Jessica have succeeded in making their virtual town *our* virtual town, and giving to the indie film and crowdfunding communities something to talk about for years to come. Not only that, they have also put together a PDF "storybook" version of *Tilt* the Town, hyperlinked and complete with the Google Map, all 170 backer bios, locations, and even an index for easily finding specific backers or aspects of *Tilt* the Town that someone may be interested in learning more about, except where the secrets are buried; that's for when we watch the film.

HOW DO YOU DIRECT
[A GARY KING MUSICAL]
— BUILD YOUR BRAND

CHAPTER FIFTY-FOUR OF THE *Tao Te Ching* tells us that by cultivating virtue, or *Te*, in oneself, virtue becomes real. At the beginning of *Batman Begins*, Ra's al Ghul tells an angry Bruce Wayne, "If you make yourself more than just a man, if you devote yourself to an ideal, you become something else entirely." Many times through this book I've stated that people give to people, but that is only partially true. People give to people who present themselves as something more than mere men and women because of their devotion to their projects, an intense passion for filmmaking, or their own urge to leave a mark on the world. In being this type of person, you are not only a filmmaker or a crowdfunder anymore. You become a brand, which can be a powerful tool, when properly used, to achieve your crowdfunding goal and much more.

Gary King ran two successful Kickstarter campaigns for his feature-length movie musical *How Do You Write a Joe Schermann Song* The first pulled in $31,101 for its initial production funds, and the second yielded $18,031 in completion funds, mainly so Gary could record a live orchestra playing the songs featured in the film. At the time, running two campaigns for the same project was seldom done, and not very successful. Now it's fairly commonplace, though success still rests in how one runs these campaigns. Gary is a master at branding and marketing, but beneath it all is a humility that keeps him grounded, and that allows him to present his brand as an extension of himself, because that's exactly what his brand is: himself. Part of this Gary King brand is innovation, but Gary's not only innovative in his crowdfunding circles. He's been innovative since the first day he picked up a camera as a kid and decided he wanted to tell stories in the medium of the movies. In the years that followed, he simply amplified this resolve and married his passion for art to the commerce that gets it made. When most filmmakers stray away from the business part of show business, Gary embraces it and more importantly, uses it for his own gain and the benefit of his audience.

THE FIRST *JOE SCHERMANN* CAMPAIGN

During Gary's first campaign, when crowdfunding was still relatively new, he made sure to follow in the footsteps of contemporary success stories like *Jens Pulver: Driven* and *Cerise*. Gary made a very personal pitch video in which he is simply being himself and casually tells viewers about his idea for his movie musical. He even delves into exactly why he wants to direct a musical more in the vein of *Rent* and *Chicago* than the film *Once*. From his *Flash Gordon* T-shirt to his little cat gazing into the camera, the pitch gives us information, a sense of Gary's world, and a smile.

Gary also had a lot of help in his initial crowdfunding campaign for *How Do You Write a Joe Schermann Song*. One of the main people by his side from crowdfunding through completion has been his lead actress, Christina Rose. She not only promoted the campaign just as much as Gary did across the social networks, but she also costarred in Gary's pitch video singing songs alongside Joe Schermann, the film's lead actor and songwriter. This also gives us a sense of a tight-knit *connection*, not only between Gary and his actors, but Gary and his backers, which is another selling point in Gary's personal brand. Not every director can get his or her actors to endorse a project, let alone help crowdfund it.

Aside from Gary's pitch for his first Kickstarter campaign, he also put in a lot of promotion time, reaching out to film websites and blogs and asking if they might help spread the word about his campaign, as well as constantly keeping his backers updated; Gary posted a total of forty-four updates to all of his 239 contributors. For Gary, *consistency* is key.

But like any campaign, a "Lull" is inevitable, and it was during such a time that Gary and Christina got together and came up with an idea to revitalize the campaign. Members of the *Joe Schermann* cast would sing and perform a song in a video at the request of any backer who pledged $300 or more. "It brought in a lot of money," Gary told me, and it made six backers quite happy. So the innovation didn't stop for a moment through this crowdfunding campaign. As mentioned in Chapter Twenty-Four, a "Lull" can be viewed as simply taking the time necessary to reevaluate the direction of your campaign and make interesting, engaging choices on how to continue it and keep its momentum on the rise.

The Second *Joe Schermann* Campaign

By the time Gary began his next crowdfunding campaign for the same project, he was seeking the funds needed to hire a sixty-piece orchestra to record all the songs for *How Do You Write a Joe Schermann Song*. By this time, the Internet was much more saturated with crowdfunding campaigns of all kinds. Like any brand name with some new competition encroaching on the market and the possibility of it stealing some of his campaign's shine, Gary changed up his game and did a few things differently this time around.

One of the main things Gary changed was keeping his backers a little less updated than he did in his previous campaign. Compare those forty-four backer updates in his first to the mere ten in the next. Gary's rationale was that since it is essentially the same campaign, he didn't want to add to the already intense campaign saturation by constantly promoting and giving backer updates on a daily or weekly basis. Instead, he kept his backers informed only about significant news regarding the progress of the campaign. Gary also continued with some tactics that worked in his prior campaign and modified others, evidenced in a "Reward Update" Gary posted, which announced that his team was compiling a list of words that Joe Schermann would incorporate into a song to be performed by members of the cast.

An interesting choice Gary made was deciding to keep his perks the same as they were in his original campaign one year before this one was launched, the idea being that the perks would still be relevant to new backers just joining the *Joe Schermann* campaign. For prior backers, as Gary mentions in his pitch video, their current pledge amount would be added to their previous pledge amount so they could qualify for a higher reward, which was a pretty risky tactic, but one that seemed to work out just fine with a whopping 244 backers pledging to this second campaign.

Keeping with the theme of personalization from the original campaign, Gary's pitch is just as personal, and this time includes lead actress Christina Rose seated beside him on a couch talking to the viewer with Gary. One aspect of this pitch that struck me as truly brilliant is Gary demonstrating what the music would sound like if it were recorded with a full sixty-piece orchestra versus only a small assortment of instruments, and that was one of his stronger selling points. That's one of the reasons I jumped on board — the orchestration sounded excellent, and I wanted Gary to have a chance to get that kind of sound for his movie.

According to Gary, the first campaign was about outreach by spreading the word about the *Joe Schermann* Kickstarter campaign to a wide array of individuals who might help bring in the funds needed to make the film. The focus of his second campaign shifted from getting in touch with bloggers and film websites and constant promotion to making the campaign more interactive for prior and potential backers alike. Because of the aforementioned "overcrowding" of campaigns

"The Pose" that helped Gary King launch over two thousand "Likes" between his three most well-known films.

streaming past our Twitter and Facebook feeds, it may not have been enough for Gary, Christina, and the indie film community to Tweet and retweet the same Tweets just to have them get lost in a flood of countless others. Like any brand worth believing in, you have to stand out.

Minimal Risk = Minimal Reward

Perhaps one of the most interesting things about Gary and his two campaigns for *How Do You Write a Joe Schermann Song* is the fact that never once was he afraid to take a risk or try something new, something that no one else had attempted. Much the way it is in filmmaking, so it goes with crowdfunding. There are risks involved, especially when you choose Kickstarter over Indiegogo or go for "Fixed" over "Flexible Funding" with Indiegogo. But as a crowdfunder, you simply can't afford to think of the risks. You have got to take them, but in a smart way, like Gary did. You have to be innovative, personable, and unwavering in your desire to get your film funded.

BELIEF IS AN ADDICTION

In a post called "Lessons Learned in the Land of Crowdfunding," which Gary wrote for his blog An Indie Life, Gary outlines all the important takeaways he received after his first campaign, which he then incorporated into his second. One of those most important ones is to "believe in yourself and your project." That's how you not only build a product like *How Do You Write a Joe Schermann Song, What's Up Lovely*, or *New York Lately*, two prior films written, directed, and self-financed by the New York City-based filmmaker, but how you build a brand like Gary King: you have to show you care not only about the product, but every aspect of it, from the writing to the cast and crew, all the way down to the audience itself.

Therefore, when we see a likeable, charismatic person like Gary and we listen to what he or she has to say, that person may become even more captivating because of the things he or she says or believes in. These kinds of people bring out the best in us. Sometimes we admire them for their passion and drive, and that builds not only respect, but also a following. We root for these people. It almost doesn't matter whether we like the final products because we appreciate the fact that the creators followed their dreams from starting gun to finish line and now have something to show for all that time and effort spent crowdfunding, writing, shooting, and editing.

That's how you build [a Gary King musical]. That's how you build a brand of jeans that anyone would want to wear.

Trignosis #3

• • •

"I Supported Cerise" and What I Got Was an Acrostic Poem!

WHEN I DECIDED TO TRY CROWDFUNDING with my short film *Cerise*, I had a lot of insecurities. Not about me, though. I knew that I had written a very solid script, following most of the rules I'd learned from my prior experience in writing short films, plus incorporating new tips I'd taken away from screenwriting books. And the insecurities weren't necessarily about crowdfunding, even though at first I was hesitant to put my film project and myself on the line and ask people for money to help me make it. After all, I did make six other short films on my own dime.

No, what I was mostly concerned about was whether I'd be able to keep it all going, in terms of promotion and fundraising, and keep my potential contributors, friends, and followers fully engaged with my campaign. I was afraid that my team and I wouldn't have the stamina it takes to keep up with the fast-paced nature of crowdfunding and innovate on a whim. Ironically, those are the areas that the crowdfunding campaign for *Cerise* became most praised for — community engagement, innovation, and dare I say it, originality, not to mention that it was one of the most personalized campaigns during a time before the crowdfunding bubble had burst.

Failure: F-A-I — I'm Sorry, I Can't Spell that Word

Much of the success crowdfunding *Cerise* was because my team and I were not afraid to fail. Well, let me backtrack a moment — *I* was very afraid to fail, which is why only a few moments before the campaign's launch I got cold feet and was about to delete it entirely and make my short the way I've done in the past. My cold feet warmed up because of Danae Ringelmann and Indiegogo's support, the prowess of my team, and of course, trial and error. In that sense, we were never afraid to try anything. For instance, one of this campaign's more popular perks was the acrostic poem for funders at the $10 level. Originally, this perk was only going to be a shout-out on Facebook and Twitter, but my team and I realized that it wasn't very engaging or personal. Then Marinell mentioned that since *Cerise* is a short film about words, and because I'm a poet, I should write every contributor at the $10 level an acrostic poem, in which every line of the poem begins with a letter of the individual funder's name.

My fear, of course, would be that I'd have to write fifty or eighty poems. And how much more difficult would it be coming up with a ten-line poem for "Alexandria" than a haiku for "Jon." Despite my reservations, we went with the idea. I'd write the poems, Marinell would format them nicely with Photoshop, and then we'd post the poems to the funders' Facebook walls, Twitpic them, or email them to those funders who didn't have a Facebook profile. The result? Very happy contributors who clicked "Like" and always commented about how beautiful the poem was, and how it brightened up their walls and their lives.

By the campaign's end, I had written nearly 120 acrostic poems of all different lengths and subject matter. Yes, it was hard work, but the reactions from our funders more than made up for the hours spent jotting down the right combination of words to best represent *Cerise*'s contributors.

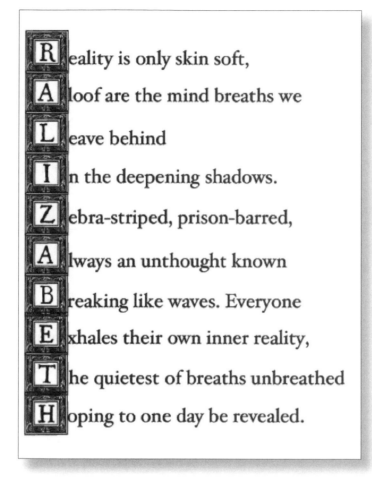

R eality is only skin soft,

A loof are the mind breaths we

L eave behind

I n the deepening shadows.

Z ebra-striped, prison-barred,

A lways an unthought known

B reaking like waves. Everyone

E xhales their own inner reality,

T he quietest of breaths unbreathed

H oping to one day be revealed.

The acrostic poem I wrote for "Ralizabeth," in which every line starts with a letter of her name.

CERISE IS A SYNONYM FOR "SAY CHEESE!"

Now that we had our community's attention, we had to hold onto its attention, because, although every day we'd receive more followers on Twitter and more friends on Facebook, people can no longer harp too long on the one thing that made them successful. They've got to show they can be innovative, as well. So my team and I thought to try and get our funders involved in the action. Marinell suggested we ask each of *Cerise*'s contributors to take a photo of him- or herself holding a sign that reads "I supported *Cerise*" and send it to us so we could post it on the *Cerise* Facebook page. I was slightly more cynical back then and didn't think that many people would actually take the time to do this. Then Marinell snapped a photo of herself holding an "I supported *Cerise*" sign, and I was sold.

It took a while before the photos started coming in, but when they did, we were pleased. The first few were pretty standard. Then we started getting others from some pretty creative funders like Cielito Pascual, who's holding up her sign in the snow with the word "cerise" etched onto the window of a car buried in the blizzard, and Frank Guzman, who spelt the word out across his floor using random items he found in his home. After a while, there seemed to be a friendly competition between *Cerise*'s contributors to see who could be the most creative in their sign-making abilities. Now that's community engagement.

We further evolved the "I supported *Cerise*" concept with videos of some of our backers, mainly those who live in the tri-state area, telling us why they chose to support my short film. The first of our participants was Andrew Bichler at Two Guys Pizza and Grill. We then caught up with Kim and Matt Garland and Matt Shea in the hallway of Arlington Lanes after an intense few games of bowling. Finally, we interviewed friend and filmmaker Raul Garcia at a gathering at Marinell's house. This proved to be quite a testament to *Cerise*, since these contributors were able to give honest feedback as to why they supported this film, which ranged from the film sounding like an interesting story to the mentioning of specific perks we offered, as well as praise for our hands-on community engagement tactics.

Due to our acrostic poems for all of our contributors, the "I supported *Cerise*" photo and video initiatives, as well as my intense amount of promotion on the social media front, *Cerise*'s campaign quickly landed itself on the Indiegogo home page where even more people

The "I Supported Cerise*" photo collage was a much bigger success than the* Cerise *team could've ever hoped it to be.*

could view our page and contribute — people we didn't already know, but whom we would treat as though we'd known all our lives. That's the mantra behind what made this campaign truly successful.

"Tried and Failed? Try Again."

Whenever you try everything, you're bound to find something that doesn't quite work out the way you wanted, and *Cerise*'s crowd-funding campaign was no exception to this rule. My team and I tried a few things that didn't engage our community like we'd hoped they would, such as the spelling twee I mentioned in an earlier chapter, in which a Twibbon would be appended to the winner's Twitter avatar, as a sign of support for *Cerise*. The only people engaged were

Marinell, Julie and Jessica from King is a Fink, and myself, as well as the occasional hashtag drifter who might stumble upon on our little #spellingbee.

On the upside, we also kept people engaged with video updates during and long after the campaign for *Cerise* had ended, being that our funders and random people seemed to get a kick out of watching me talk about *Cerise*, then segue off to some other semi-related topic, somehow getting back to the point within a two- or three-minute timespan. Continuing in this tradition, the *Cerise* team and I started holding video contests. Some of them were for everyone, like our "Tagline Contest," in which we attempted to crowdsource a tagline for the film. Others were for funders only, as an added thanks for their contribution, as exemplified by a couple of random giveaways Marinell and I held, handing off DVD copies of my previous films to selected members of the *Cerise* community.

Cerise's Indiegogo campaign was active at a time when crowdfunding was only starting to become a legitimate alternative for funding one's film. Our online community of filmmakers and crowdfunders would watch the campaigns for *Tilt*, *How Do You Write a Joe Schermann Song*, *Solomon Grundy*, and many others flourish, and it's humbling to know that many of the crowdfunders behind these films cite the *Cerise* campaign as one that helped fuel their own drive and foster their crowdfunding creativity and originality. But make no mistake: as with *Cerise* and the majority of the campaigns mentioned in this book, successful crowdfunding is about personalization, innovation, and not being afraid to do whatever it takes to succeed. It's impossible to know what will work and what won't, so you shouldn't be hesitant to try any- and everything, then keep what works, ditch what doesn't, and repeat as needed.

...

Synced Up with Details and Nostalgia

AS MENTIONED VERY EARLY ON there is no foolproof way to go about crowdfunding for your indie film, but as long as you have one or two interesting and innovative things going on in your campaign, you'll most likely come out on top. A great example of this is the campaign for the short film *Sync*, which found crowdfunding success on Indiegogo by raising $405 over its initial goal of $3,000 through a masterfully executed campaign spearheaded by Seattle-based filmmaker Brendon Fogle.

Remember When... The Power of Nostalgia

Brendon starts out with a standard, personal pitch video. He then goes a step further and shares a question with his potential funders — "Do you remember the first album you ever bought?" — and then a brief story about the first album he ever got and the feeling it gave him to hold a CD in his hand as opposed to downloading music onto an MP3 player. This intro sets the tone of the movie's *storyline* brilliantly — *Sync* revolves around a grandfather who's trying to connect with his MP3ed-in grandson through the gift of records. As for perks, Brendon starts off with one of the more typical ones: stickers. And although they're very cool stickers, they're a ruse, because the architecture of the *Sync* campaign reveals a "Sweet Spot" of truly exceptional, personalized perks further down the line.

As he was planning out his Indiegogo campaign, Brendon was sure about one thing: he wanted to create a product and campaign that was fun, and he also wanted to offer perks that not only movie fans would enjoy. Therefore, holding on tight to the theme of vinyl and the overlaying concept of nostalgia, Brendon offered a piece of himself starting at the $33 perk level by giving funders a record from his very own record collection.

It's a personal perk like this that can mean the difference between funders settling for a sticker at $12 or upping their contribution so they can receive something truly memorable and even more tangible. That's what did it for me when I became a proud funder of *Sync*, as I mentioned earlier. I wondered just what record I might get, and I was very pleased when I received *Sammy Davis Jr.'s Greatest Hits* in the mail two weeks later, as well as my sticker, of course.

The nostalgia factor doesn't stop at receiving a record from Brendon's own personal collection. At $78, Brendon turns his attention from crowdfunder to Photoshop artist, turning photos of *Sync*'s mild-mannered funders into super-hip album covers. By giving a photograph what Brendon calls the "Blue Note Treatment," he transforms that old Christmas photo of you into a vintage-looking record from the 1960s.

THE DESIRE'S IN THE DETAILS

Besides these hip and original perks at the $33 and $78 levels — what Brendon calls the "Sweet Spot" — snuggly placed between the more standard perks of shout-outs and stickers ($3 – $12), T-shirts and producer credits ($128 – $256), what also stands out in Brendon's campaign for *Sync* is his impeccable attention to detail. For instance, each perk has its own nifty title attached to it. "Delicious Vinyl," "33 1/3 RPMazing," and "Bad Mama Gramophone" are neat, fun titles that add a lighthearted feel to Brendon's campaign. Then, when you read the descriptions of the perks, they are not only humorous and airy, but play on the idea of vinyl and records, as in Brendon's $12 perk: "Side A: All of the above. Side B: Plus a digital download of the film, and a *Sync* sticker (perfect for pimping your laptop or Trapper Keeper."

Sync's "Blue Note Treatment" on one of my own photos magically turns it into a vintage album cover from the 1960s.

Also, as you've no doubt already noticed, the perk amounts are not the standard $5 and $50 amounts, but instead are based on record RPMs, like 12, 33, and 78, for instance. What about the $3 perk level, which grants funders a spot on *Sync's* "playlist" and a thank you in the end credits of the film? That's a play on "MP3." Everything in Brendon's campaign is relevant to the film's content and storyline, making for a more engaging experience from day one to deadline's end.

THE VANCE CONNORS TAPES

Amidst all of Brendon's masterfully crafted campaigning for *Sync*, there comes Vance Connors. Who is Vance Connors, you ask? He's

Brendon's alter ego, ace in the hole, and an ingenious way to help drive more traffic to *Sync*'s Indiegogo page and keep fresh content flowing through Brendon's Facebook and Twitter channels. Brendon grew up watching late night infomercials, and, thinking back to those nostalgic days, the idea to create his own infomercials dawned on him. It would serve as an interesting, relevant way to explain the perks he was offering and keep the campaign playful and immediate. Thus, Vance Connors was born, taking inspiration from celebrity endorsers like Tony Little, Ron Popeil, and Billy Blanks, who lit up his living room at three in the morning back when there were fewer than 2,000 channels to watch on the television set.

Vance Connors — Sync *spokesperson and all-around hepcat.*

That's Brendon starring as Vance in three videos in which he introduces his $12, $33, and $78 perks. The videos are as vintage as many of the other aspects of *Sync*'s campaign, and include brightly colored backgrounds over which Vance is superimposed, cheesy graphics, and video noise synonymous with 1980s analog technology. The details are what make this campaign a memorable one instead of only a memory.

It's Brendon's attention to the details and commitment to his film project and campaign that made *Sync*'s time in the crowdfunding arena both entertaining and successful. It's this kind of fine scrutiny that potential funders want to see, with elements from your film connected all the way through your campaign. Whatever the genre, mood, and tone of your film might be, you should strive to make every dot of your campaign connect to every dot of your film so it all counts for something special and stands the test of time.

...

STUCK LIKE CHUCK, TOO: THE INDIE SEQUEL THAT COULDN'T AND WHY

THERE HAVE BEEN MANY monumental successes for DIY filmmakers who have turned to crowdfunding to help make their films a reality. There have also been projects that unfortunately have not seen even a modicum of success in this arena. This is understandable, as it keeps crowdfunding in balance; you can't have one without the other. It gets more difficult to understand exactly why a campaign has not been successful when the crowdfunder has seemingly done everything in his or her power to get the word out about the campaign, but still comes up short.

One such case is the Indiegogo campaign for Jerry Cavallaro's indie sequel *Stuck Like Chuck, Too*, which attempted to raise $15,000 and only brought in $2,500 in three months of fundraising. But the reason for this campaign's foundering is not for lack of trying. I watched intently as the *Stuck Like Chuck, Too* campaign gained momentum. I watched as Jerry put out Tweet upon Tweet, and zealously shared his campaign on Facebook. And even on FilmSnobbery, the Internet talk show Jerry cohosts with Nic Baisley, there was never a moment when Jerry didn't mention either *Stuck Like Chuck*, his first feature-length romantic comedy, which went on to screen at the Orlando Film Festival, or his campaign for the sequel he hoped to produce.

In an article written by Paul Osborne and published by *MovieMaker* magazine called "A Film in the Crowd," Jerry speaks out about his unsuccessful campaign with *Stuck Like Chuck, Too*:

I wish I knew why my campaign failed. I treated it as a full-time job. I utilized social media in a big way and spent at least eight hours every day promoting the project online. I went to film festivals, screenings, panels and even some charity events in New York to promote my campaign in person. I did everything to get the project out there. Unfortunately, in the end, it was nowhere near enough.

While all of this may be true, it still remains a mystery to Jerry as to why his campaign didn't even reach 25% of his fundraising goal. Perhaps it's not what Jerry didn't do, but rather what he did do that may have been the drawback. Let's delve into a few aspects of Jerry's *Stuck Like Chuck, Too* Indiegogo campaign that I think were detrimental.

NameTag Line

The first thing that catches my eye is the image on Jerry's pitch video. It's a nametag, with which Jerry gained fame and an "Indie Spirit" award at Orlando Film Festival for promoting *Stuck Like Chuck* by walking around wearing a giant pillow-shaped costume that read, "Hello, *I'm Stuck Like Chuck*." The only addition to the nametag from the original film is the word "*Too*" appended after it, bold and off-centered to make it apparent that it was written in. None of this is a

The first thing a potential funder sees on the Stuck Like Chuck, Too *Indiegogo page should be anything but pointless.*

problem, though. The problem is the tag line beneath the nametag: "Not a sequel but just as pointless."

Initially, one might see this as a fun and quirky little slogan. The fact is, however, that Jerry was asking strangers to pitch in some money and help raise the pretty substantial sum of $15,000 for a "pointless" film. Why would anyone want to throw his or her hard-earned cash away on a "pointless" project? Obviously, Jerry doesn't mean to say that his film is worthless in any way. Honestly, if most crowdfunders (and filmmakers in general) showed half as much passion and drive for their projects as Jerry had done with *Stuck Like Chuck, Too*, they would all run successful campaigns due to that level of devotion and charisma alone. However, Jerry was trying to architect his crowdfunding campaign around the central themes and genre of the film, which is a very youthful, romantic comedy featuring lots of self-deprecating humor reflected not only in the *Stuck Like Chuck, Too* tag line, but also in just about everything else related to the campaign. This is where the problems arose.

THE FINE LINE BETWEEN FUNNY AND F'ED UP

One thing to really avoid, even in jest, is insulting your potential contributors, which may be a surefire reason why Jerry was only able to bring in $2,500 of a $15,000 goal. Your contributors don't have to contribute to your crowdfunding campaign. When they do, they become the most wonderful and important people in the world and should be treated as such at all times, especially *before* they actually contribute.

Jerry's lowest amount for contributing to *Stuck Like Chuck, Too*'s campaign is $1, which is pretty standard in most campaigns. But the first sentence of the perk description, "Wow, you are a cheap bastard," is pretty severe, even though it's meant strictly for comedic effect. As a contributor who just gave a filmmaker a few dollars of my weekly paycheck, I don't think I'd want to be called a "cheap bastard," even in jest, and especially if I've had a particularly rough day at the office. The blow is unsuccessfully feathered with "just kidding" following right after, but it's the initial impact that won't be so easily forgotten.

The $500 and $1,000 perks get a bit more verbose. Although throughout his perks Jerry plays with iconic names like "Lloyd Kaufman" and "Rainn Wilson" as perk titles, then plays them up further within the perk descriptions, if you've never seen the movies he's referring to, you could be lost and even offended. Take the "Jake Gyllenhaal" perk, for instance, which reads, "Thank you for donating the FIVE HUNDRED DOLLAH! that the crazy Asian guy gave you for your Bubble Boy wedding." If you didn't see *Bubble Boy*, this could come across as pretty harsh, especially if you're Asian and don't have much of a sense of humor. My personal favorite is the "Gary Busey," stating that this $1,000 perk is "just as batshit crazy as you are."

While it's definitely a positive thing to incorporate some fun elements and a fair amount of humor into a crowdfunding campaign for a romantic comedy, you should make sure the comedy comes across in the right way. I've met Jerry and have hung out with him on many occasions, and I will attest to the fact that he's very comical in person. That humor, however, doesn't necessarily come across in his campaign when read by people who look at it armed with their own preconceived thoughts, ideas, and opinions.

PERSONALIZATION: MORE FISHES CALLED FUNDERS

A deeper look at Jerry's perks for the *Stuck Like Chuck, Too* campaign reveals that there is really nothing personal about them. They are standard fare: a personal thank you, a music sampler, associate and executive producer credit, VIP passes to film festivals, and DVD copies of the original *Stuck Like Chuck*. There is one limited-time perk that's partial to filmmakers at the $50 "Tina Fey" level, in which a funder will get half off on a submission fee to the Orlando Film Festival, which unfortunately ignores any non-filmmakers contributing at this substantial level. Jerry does get innovative and original, but way too late in the game at $1,000, in which he'll buy a goldfish and name it after the funder who contributed at the "batshit crazy" level.

That said, what Jerry's campaign could have benefited greatly from was not so much comedy, but personalization in every aspect of it. Little bits here and there would have gone a long way. A few more goldfish perks a bit lower on the perk ladder nearer the $20 level. People sometimes need a larger incentive than helping a struggling indie filmmaker make his or her film. Plus, the fact that Jerry was able to make the original *Stuck Like Chuck* for mere pocket change and is now asking for $15,000 may have been a bit of a deterrent for many people, especially since *Stuck Like Chuck, Too* was going to be shot in much the same fashion as the original.

It's also interesting to note that Jerry's original goal was for $30,000, mostly for "travel costs, locations, food, props, wardrobe, music, cast, crew (except [Jerry]), new equipment, SAG, E & O, insurance, our awesome celebrity cameos and anything else related to the production," according to Jerry.

PLAN B (FOR WHEN NO ONE SEEMS TO CARE)

One final aspect of Jerry's *Stuck Like Chuck, Too* campaign, and any other campaigns that raise little or none of their target amounts, is the fact that no matter how much you promote, no matter how stellar your pitch video or how personal your perks may be, sometimes people just don't care about your project. This is a very difficult truth to accept, but a look at Jerry's pitch video demonstrates a dry sense of humor and little passion for his project, which is simply not the case. That kind of a pitch, intercut with clips from the previous *Stuck Like Chuck*, may not have been enough to make someone care about the project he's crowdfunding for.

Case in point: Osborne's article mentions that the *Stuck Like Chuck, Too* campaign "received nearly 22,000 views, making it one of the most sampled active projects in the history of Indiegogo, according to Slava Rubin, the site's co-founder." But these outstanding numbers did not equate to a crowdfunding victory for Jerry. Compare that with *Cerise's* 6,930 campaign views, which translated to $6,300 in funds raised from 117 funders.

Getting people to emotionally invest in your project and ultimately to contribute to your crowdfunding campaign begins with you. You have to show them you care, that this film is your life. But in the event that passion is not enough, you should always have backup plans, as Gary King mentions in the same article in *MovieMaker* magazine:

> If you want to make your film then definitely don't let the campaign be the make or break of it. At the end of the day, know that you are going to make your film no matter what. I had a Plan B in place for if my Kickstarter campaign didn't succeed. That's just being smart.

This is solid advice and should be heeded. But the other option is one that my good friend, nonfiction writer James Broderick, employs when sending out queries for book proposals to various publishers. If he gets them all back and no one is interested, he tosses the idea aside and moves on to the next idea and gives that one a try. Therefore, if you as a filmmaker don't find the kind of success you expected to find by crowdfunding Project A, and if you're not fully invested in Project A, move on to Project B with newfound knowledge to use in your next crowdfunding campaign. Ultimately, you will have a film project that people will care enough about to help make happen.

Conclusion

• • •

THE *YOU* OF CROWDFUNDING

IT'S HARD WORK MAKING A MOVIE. It's harder work securing the funding to make one. And even though online fundraising
has afforded many creatives the most accessible bridge connecting
first draft to finished product, it's still hard work to architect and
maintain an engaging and appealing crowdfunding campaign. The
good news is that, as filmmakers, in particular, we don't have to be
Kevin Smith or the next Ed Burns to acquire the money we need to
turn our script pages into screen frames.

The ways we crowdfund will undoubtedly change in the years to
come, especially in light of United States legislation like the JOBS
Act. Laws like this can dramatically shift the landscape of crowdfunding for better or worse. Successful crowdfunding is no exact science
and may forever exist in a perpetual state of trial and error. It's only
because of past victories that we know as much as we do about
what works best and what can be detrimental for a film campaign.
This is why *Crowdfunding for Filmmakers* is full of specific examples from
projects that have found success by trying, possibly failing, then trying
something different, and repeating the cycle all over again in the
next crowdfunding campaign.

One important truth to keep in mind is that raising money online
for your film project is very similar to Tweeting about a screening of
your recent short at a local festival or getting people to "Like" your
movie on Facebook. At the end of the day, the *Tao* of crowdfunding
is the "Way" of publicity, and today, "publicity" really means being
a person before a petition, or saying hello before asking for money.
Even the world's leading companies are turning toward social networking for maximum outreach, but you don't have to be a Taoist

master to see they're going about it more socially than traditional advertising dictates. There's now a face behind most companies, someone who's extending a virtual hand to embrace yours in a Digital Age handshake that will welcome you further into the fold of his or her product. That's what crowdfunding your project should be like, too, but it seldom starts with the Do-It-Yourself filmmaker, the 24fps dreamer, or the aspiring movie actor. It usually begins with the *real* you.

It's quite easy to disregard this fact, and if you do, don't panic — it doesn't necessarily mean you won't reach your crowdfunding goal. But remember this: crowdfunding is not only about raising money, but also about building your audience for this film and your future projects. Therefore, we should let go of all the misconceptions about film financing — how it's supposed to be secured by suit-and-tie producers and investors with no care for your film's artistic integrity, or paid for out-of-pocket — and instead accept the fact that we are the ones now responsible for acquiring that funding. As filmmakers, we are not only artists, but entrepreneurs as well, and we would do well to keep these two fundamental forces in balance at all times.

The tools for crowdfunding your next short or feature-length film, web series, or video project are all here in this book — from choosing the right platform to expertly navigating the social media spectrum. No matter what technological innovations or legislative measures evolve to further enhance online fundraising, the essence of successful crowdfunding will remain firmly rooted in the soil of personalization, and the heart of your crowdfunding campaign will always lie with you.

Appendix

Some Memorable Pitch Videos

Before pointing you to what I consider to be some really memorable pitch videos for successfully crowdfunded film projects, I'm including my own pitch for *Cerise* as a textbook example of the kind of pitch I speak about throughout *Crowdfunding for Filmmakers*. If you have a smart phone with a QR code scanner app installed, you can simply scan the QR code below the campaign description and view the pitch video directly on your phone. If not, a link to the campaign's homepage is included in the description of the film project.

Cerise
A former spelling bee champion is haunted by the word that took him down.
$6,300 raised of $5,000 goal
Indiegogo
http://www.indiegogo.com/Cerise?a=11009

Here are a few interesting, innovative, and sometimes just plain fun pitch videos from passionate and driven filmmakers who put in the extra effort to bring their pitches to life so that contributors could help them bring their films to life.

I Am I – Feature Film
A Narrative Film project in Los Angeles, CA by Jocelyn Towne
$111,965 pledged of $100,000 goal
Kickstarter
http://www.kickstarter.com/projects/2115598587/i-am-i-feature-film

Red Scare
Better Dead Than Red!
$7,645 raised of $7,500 goal
Indiegogo
http://www.youtube.com/watch?v=Z678aj1UukI&feature=player_embedded#!

Man-child – Feature Film
A Narrative Film project in Brooklyn, NY by Koo
$125,100 pledged of $115,000 goal
Kickstarter
http://www.kickstarter.com/projects/ryanbkoo/man-child-feature-film

Sound It Out: shoot
Help us finish our journey and take SOUND IT OUT to your town
$4,468 raised of $3,000 goal
Indiegogo
http://www.indiegogo.com/sound?a=11009

ThanksKilling – Killer Turkey Movie Sequel!
A Narrative Film project in Los Angeles, CA by Jordan Downey
$112,248 pledged of $100,000 goal
Kickstarter
http://www.kickstarter.com/projects/jordandowney/thankskilling-sequel-horror-comedy-feature-film

Completing the Film *Tiny Dancer*
A legendary dancer (Katherine Crockett) struggles to balance her drive for perfection on her journey to find happiness.
$10,275 raised of $9,000 goal
Indiegogo
http://www.indiegogo.com/finishingtinydancer

Misdirected
A Film & Video project in Los Angeles, CA by Lauren Mora
$6,000 pledged of $5,000 goal
Kickstarter
www.kickstarter.com/projects/557072821/misdirected

ADDITIONAL RESOURCES FOR CROWDFUNDERS

Crowdfunding for Filmmakers will no doubt prove an invaluable asset to help get you through a crowdfunding campaign, whether it's your first time fundraising online, or you're a seasoned crowdfunder in need of a refresher course. It's always a good idea to keep up to date with the future of crowdfunding. Stay in the know about which new projects are making waves across the indie film community and examine how those campaigners are achieving innovation and success. But this in itself can be quite laborious.

Luckily, most filmmakers who finish a crowdfunding campaign usually take some time to write a brief blog post that explores what they've learned from their campaigning, what they would've done differently, what definitely worked, and, more times than not, how they never thought crowdfunding would require as much time and effort as it does. It's in your best interest to keep a keen eye on film campaigns for movies like yours and be sure to read those insightful afterthoughts about crowdfunding.

To make it easier, a good friend of mine named Bella Wonder, who runs a blog site called Wonderland, has compiled a very comprehensive list of blog posts from fellow filmmakers who've launched successful and not-so-successful crowdfunding campaigns. It's been aptly named "The Crowdfunder's Bible," and includes my original *Tao of Crowdfunding* blog post "Three Ps for a Successful Film Campaign." It also features many bits of sagely insight from crowdfunders mentioned throughout this book like Jeanie Finlay (*Sound It Out*), Meg Pinsonneault (*Gwapa (Beautiful)*), and Gary King (*How Do You Write a Joe Schermann Song*), and plenty of others who've seen crowdfunding success, such as Oklahoma Ward, who raised $10,352 of his $10,000 Kickstarter goal for a documentary on the making of two hardcore indie horror films, *Crawl Bitch Crawl* (directed by Ward himself) and *Screen* (directed by David Paul Baker) and David Branin, who raised $16,203 of a $15,000 goal on Kickstarter for his feature-length film *Goodbye Promise*.

You can find Bella's "Crowdfunder's Bible" here: *http://bellawonder. com/the-crowdfunders-bible/*

Another solid source for assistance is RocketHub's own "Crowdfunding Manifesto," located on the website's blog at *http://rockethub. org/page/manifesto-strategy*. The manifesto was created by RocketHub CEO Brian Meece and serves to instruct crowdfunders of all kinds in the basics of online fundraising by focusing on three main "pillars" for success: The Project, The Network, and The Rewards. Although the "Crowdfunding Manifesto" is not film-centric, it covers all one needs to know in order to run a successful campaign for anything, creative or otherwise.

Then, of course, there's Ted Hope's Indiewire blog Hope for Film, which occasionally features informative posts pertaining to crowdfunding. In fact, Indiegogo's Principal/Business Developer Adam Chapnick, who is also CEO of Distribber, worked with Ted to feature a batch of Indiegogo success stories (*Cerise* included) during the 2011 Toronto International Film Festival. Indiegogo and Kickstarter, as well, offer useful blogs, informative Q&A segments, and video interviews on their respective websites, which are extremely helpful for crowdfunders at every level of experience.

For information strictly about crowdfunding and crowdsourcing, there are these three powerhouses the first two of which I mentioned in Chapter Thirty-four: The Daily Crowdsource (*http://dailycrowdsource. com/*), *www.crowdsourcing.org*, and *www.CrowdFundingHelp.com*, three websites that offer excellent insider tips on how to crowdfund smarter, not harder. *www.crowdsourcing.org* is also the home of the Crowdfunding Accreditation for Platform Standards (CAPS), which governs all crowdfunding activities under the JOBS Act. Because the content on this particular website tends toward the entrepreneurs of the world, I once again highly suggest following Daily Crowdsource on Twitter (@TDCrowdsource) for up-to-the-minute information on all things related to crowdfunding.

Finally, here is a list of a handful of other blog posts, articles, and stories — some of which have been mentioned in *Crowdfunding for Filmmakers* — that I think will also offer much insight and many helpful tips to lead you to a crowdfunding victory:

- "How to Fund a Successful Indiegogo/Kickstarter Campaign in 5 Easy Steps" by Stephen Dunn (Indiewire): *http://blogs.indiewire. com/thelostboy/how-to-fund-a-successful-indiegogo-kickstarter-campaign-in-5-easy-steps#*

- "The Etiquette of Crowdfunding: A Recipient's View" by Pete Brook (Prison Photography): *http://prisonphotography.wordpress. com/2012/01/21/the-etiquette-of-crowdfunding-a-recipients-view/*

- "Reaching Out to the Crowd: Is it Worth it to Crowdfund?" by R. C. Varenas (Film Slate): *http://www.filmslatemagazine.com/blog/ reaching-out-to-the-crowd-is-it-worth-it-to-crowdfund*

- "The Newbie's Guide to Social Networking" by Meg Pinson-neault (Film Courage): *http://filmcourage.com/node/833*

- "A Film in the Crowd" by Paul Osborne (*MovieMaker*): *http://www.moviemaker.com/producing/article/crowdfunding_kick-starter_indiegogo_case_studies_20110427/*

- "Maximizing Distribution Through Crowdfunding" by Peter Broderick (Hope for Film): *http://blogs.indiewire.com/tedhope/max-imizing-distribution-through-crowdfunding?utm_source=feedburner&utm_medium=feed*

- "5 Sobering Realities of Crowd-Funding" by Princeton Holt (Film Courage): *http://www.filmcourage.com/content/5-sobering-realities-crowd-funding*

- "7 Reasons Why Crowdfunding Projects Fail" by Justin Kown-acki (CrowdFundingHelp): *http://crowdfundinghelp.com/7-reasons-why-crowdfunding-projects-fail/*

BIBLIOGRAPHY

Fractured Atlas. "Fiscal Sponsorship: About Fiscal Sponsorship." *http://www.fracturedatlas.org/site/fiscal/*

Holt, Princeton. "5 Sobering Realties of Crowdfunding." Film Courage. Last modified November 14, 2011. *http://www.filmcourage.com/content/5-sobering-realities-crowd-funding*

Margolis, Michael. *Believe Me: Why Your Vision, Brand and Leadership Need a Bigger Story*. New York: Get Storied Press, 2009. PDF edition.

Osborne, Paul. "A Film in the Crowd." *MovieMaker*. Last modified April 15, 2011. *http://www.moviemaker.com/producing/page2/crowdfunding_kickstarter_indiegogo_case_studies_20110427/*

Smith, Nigel. "Jennifer Fox Raises $150,000 for 'My Reincarnation' on Kickstarter." Indiewire. Last modified May 31, 2011. *http://www.indiewire.com/article/spiritual_doc_my_reincarnation_bomes_top_raising_finished_film_on_kickstart#*

Tzu, Lao. *Tao Te Ching*. Translated by Gia-Fu Feng and Jane English. New York: Vintage Books, 1989.

Tzu, Sun. *The Art of War*. Translated by Lionel Giles. El Paso: El Paso Norte Press, 2005.

Wise, Eric. "Transmedia Storytelling." MasteringFilm. Accessed on May 31, 2012. *http://masteringfilm.com/transmedia-storytelling/*

ABOUT THE AUTHOR

Poet, writer, and filmmaker John T. Trigonis has published work in a variety of literary journals all over the world. In 2007 he was a nominee for a Pushcart Prize in poetry. He has self-published a number of free chapbooks, including *Androids with Angel Faces* (2005), *Warehouse City Blues* (2011), and *Warehouse City Noir* (2012).

In February of 2010, John and his team launched a crowdfunding campaign on Indiegogo for his seventh short film, *Cerise*, in which they raised a total of $6,300 — $1,300 over their initial goal of $5,000 — in only three months, solely through Facebook and Twitter. 70% of these funds came from people he'd never even met. Once the film was finished, John spearheaded a series of crowdfunding "Crusades" and raised an additional $2,000 to use to submit the film to festivals. *Cerise* has since screened at over a dozen venues, participated in the Cannes *Court Métrage*, was nominated for four awards, and won an "Award of Merit" at Indie Fest.

He's currently working on rewrites of two feature-length screen-plays and submitting a proposal for a comic book series to publishers. When not working on his creative endeavors, John helps indie film and video campaigns raise funds on Indiegogo as the company's Vertical Manager for Film, Web & Video.

You can contact John through his website/blog at
http://johntrigonis.com
and/or follow him on Twitter (@Trigonis).

PRODUCER TO PRODUCER
A STEP-BY-STEP GUIDE TO
LOW BUDGET INDEPENDENT FILM PRODUCING

MAUREEN A. RYAN

Everything you need to know – all in one place – to produce your independent film or documentary, from last year's Academy Award-winning co-producer of *Man on Wire*.

All the steps are clearly stated so that you can produce your low budget independent film. Save time and money by following the advice and information in Producer to Producer to make the most successful film possible.

This book is a definitive step-by-step guide for low budget independent film producing. Filled with practical advice award-winning producer Maureen Ryan has culled from her 20-plus years of production experience, it takes you through the entire process of bringing a film into the world. From development and script breakdown, to budgeting and preproduction, to production and post, and to sales and distribution, *Producer to Producer* gives you all the information you need in easy-to-follow, chronological order.

Emerging and professional producers alike will benefit from this comprehensive guide to low budget film producing. *Producer to Producer*, which outlines every aspect of film producing in detail, is designed to take to production meetings. It includes checklists to keep you on track from 12 weeks before shooting to the first day of principal photography and through postproduction.

"This does what no book on production has done before — you actually can go out and make a movie after you read it. Maureen Ryan is one of the best independent producers working today and this book will show you why. Like her, it's thorough, thoughtful, and highly enjoyable. Whether you are a novice or a professional, there is much to learn here."

— Ben Odell, producer, *Padre Nuestro*, partner, Panamax Films

MAUREEN RYAN has been a film producer for over 20 years with experience in narrative film, documentary, short film, commercials, music videos, and industrials. Other films she produced have won a BAFTA Award, a Peabody Award, and an Emmy nomination. She has taught film producing at Columbia University's School of the Arts Graduate Film Program since 1999 and also teaches producing at NYU's Tisch School of the Arts.

$39.95 · 350 PAGES · ORDER NUMBER 144RLS · ISBN: 9781932907759

THE MYTH OF MWP

In a dark time, a light bringer came along, leading the curious and the frustrated to clarity and empowerment. It took the well-guarded secrets out of the hands of the few and made them available to all. It spread a spirit of openness and creative freedom, and built a storehouse of knowledge dedicated to the betterment of the arts.

The essence of the Michael Wiese Productions (MWP) is empowering people who have the burning desire to express themselves creatively. We help them realize their dreams by putting the tools in their hands. We demystify the sometimes secretive worlds of screenwriting, directing, acting, producing, film financing, and other media crafts.

By doing so, we hope to bring forth a realization of 'conscious media' which we define as being positively charged, emphasizing hope and affirming positive values like trust, cooperation, self-empowerment, freedom, and love. Grounded in the deep roots of myth, it aims to be healing both for those who make the art and those who encounter it. It hopes to be transformative for people, opening doors to new possibilities and pulling back veils to reveal hidden worlds.

MWP has built a storehouse of knowledge unequaled in the world, for no other publisher has so many titles on the media arts. Please visit www.mwp.com where you will find many free resources and a 25% discount on our books. Sign up and become part of the wider creative community!

Onward and upward,

Michael Wiese
Publisher/Filmmaker